Entrepreneurship

The seeds of success

John Forbat

NEW AGE INTERNATIONAL PUBLISHERS

No responsibility for loss occasioned to any person or corporate body acting or refraining to act as a result of reading material in this book can be accepted by the Publisher, by the Author, or by the employer of the Author.

First Indian Sub-Continent Edition : 2008
by New Age International (P) Ltd., Publishers

This special low-priced edition is for sale in India, Bangladesh, Bhutan, Mayanmar (Burma), Sri Lanka, Nepal and Pakistan only.

Originally Published in the *United Kingdom*.

ISBN (10): 81-224-2251-9
ISBN (13): 978-81-224-2251-1

Original Edition Price: £ 12.99
Indian Edition Price: ₹ 200.00

C-11-08-5819

Printed in India at Parmanand Offset, Delhi.

PUBLISHING FOR ONE WORLD
NEW AGE INTERNATIONAL (P) LIMITED, PUBLISHERS
4835/24, Ansari Road, Daryaganj, New Delhi-110002
Visit us at **www.newagepublishers.com**

Contents

Biography

John Forbat was an immigrant to London from Hungary, at the age of seven. After qualifying as an aeronautical engineer, his professional life started with big companies in the aircraft and avionics industries and in the electronics industry. Those years involved highly capital and development oriented businesses, giving him the experience of how large companies are managed – and mismanaged. It also enabled him to experience the extent to which entrepreneurship can be stifled, by excessively corporatist attitudes in business. He then moved into a number of highly entrepreneurial businesses encompassing products, product innovation and services worldwide, where it became necessary to achieve the impossible – at least according to the textbooks. His successes – and few failures – taught him where the essentials of entrepreneurship lie and what the defining characteristics of entrepreneurs are.

During World War II he was probably London's youngest Fireguard. At sixteen he learned to fly gliders entirely solo and later gained a Private Pilot's Licence. He learned and practiced leadership skills as a Scout and as a Scout Leader and was also a keen sailor, skippering an open whaler from London to Calais and back with a crew of teenagers. He recently returned after living in the USA for over 20 years – and does not like taking "It's impossible" for an answer.

Preface

Who the book is for

The down to earth ideas and experiences related here should provide valuable reading to all budding entrepreneurs and practising business executives. It could be a valuable and practical addition to the curriculum of business schools and gainful reading for civil servants and their masters in Government, who have such a profound effect on the environment in which entrepreneurs have to live.

What the book covers

The purpose of this book is to apply the lessons I gleaned from practical business experiences and challenges, to the formation of the budding entrepreneur's attitude and business aspirations. His business plans can then be based on the real world, as well as on any professional management training. The following chapters relate mainly to entrepreneurship in industry and cover topics from issues for start-ups, to problems of the more complex company's chief executive. They thread an instructive path of real life, first hand case studies and developed ideas, through aspiration to success. without neglecting occasional failure and painful disappointment.

It is intended to show that entrepreneurs can successfully challenge the normally accepted limits of "what is possible" in business. Chapters relate to different aspects of entrepreneurship and go on to illustrate actual business experiences – *enumerating the lessons to be learned.*

Entrepreneurship is usually associated with individuals and small companies. Yet it is the successful entrepreneurs who develop businesses into large corporations, when it is their spirit, leadership and determination that engender continuous growth. How often does such a large corporation lose its way and its sparkle, when the original entrepreneur retires or sells out? How often does a large corporation stifle entrepreneurial promise in its employees?

Success comes only to the few and it can come to the "seat of the pants" type with sufficient luck – as it can be denied to the professionally trained and experienced ... For a chance of success, every entrepreneur needs imagination and vision, perseverance in pursuit of a dream and the capacity for sheer hard work. If success leads to a corporation style business, leadership skills and sensitivity to people become as important as the continuation of the entrepreneurial spirit.

How the book is structured

The following chapters relate mainly to entrepreneurship in industry and cover topics from issues for the young aspiring engineer, to problems of the chief executive. They narrate success and failure, hope and disappointment. Their origination from one pen tends to weave a thread, which follows particular experiences, without constituting a complete story.

A number of the chapters have been published as essays in management journals and have been adapted where desirable, for continuity. Others find their place as necessary companions.

Supporting website

A website supporting this book can be found at:
www.harriman-house.com/entrepreneurship

Acknowledgements

I would like to acknowledge the encouragement and support received over many years from Robert Heller, who published some of my articles in *Management Today* and who has written the Foreword to this book. Perhaps I should also acknowledge my many business friends, collaborators, competitors (and antagonists!) over the years, who contributed to my experiences and accumulated learning.

Dedication

This book is dedicated to Mary, my loving wife of over 50 years, who stood by me through thick and thin, without complaint or hesitation in enabling me to pursue many dreams. Her support while bringing up a large family and her endurance of some hard times have been cardinal to my ability to forge some success out of adversity.

Foreword

Entrepreneurs have never been more in fashion. In this respect, Britain has caught up with the US, where the go-getting businessman has long reigned. Now, on both sides of the Atlantic, politicians court the entrepreneurs, the media glorify them, and the public admires their wealth. The adulation has a hard core of justification. The great majority of businesses in any developed economy are entrepreneurial foundations, and it is from them that the major businesses of the future generally grow.

As John Forbat's subtitle suggests, entrepreneurship both sows the seeds of success and reaps their fruits. Yet, despite its enormous importance, this fundamental economic activity is imperfectly understood and little taught. Even the elementary facts about its vital role escape many educated people. My then publisher once objected to the subtitle I had given to a proposed new book called Goldfinger: How entrepreneurs grow rich by starting small. Plainly out of his depth, the publisher said fatuously, "But you can't do that".

Well, people can and do, and they change the world in the process. Think only of Microsoft and Google, both small start-ups that have created vast wealth. True, the failure rate is very high, and the big successes relatively rare. This may partly reflect the shortage of powerful, informed guidance, such as that provided by Forbat. Generally, successful entrepreneurs have neither the time nor the intellectual focus to organise and present the lessons learnt in their careers. Drawing on both American and British experience, Forbat has tackled the task with skill and penetration, and without shirking the cardinal fact about entrepreneurial achievement; it is seldom easy.

Success usually requires an endless amount of hard work, absolute concentration, and perseverance through thick and thin. Forbat pulls no punches on this issue. I once launched a newsletter called Business Fast Lane, which was aimed at would-be entrepreneurs. It had a wonderful response from potential subscribers, rapidly followed by an equally memorable flood of cancellations. These people, it seemed, were Walter Mittys, dreamers who were deeply shocked to discover how much stern effort is required, and over just how many different areas of activity.

Those reading this admirable book will not be in the dark on either proposition. Forbat takes the reader on a logical path, starting with what you need to learn, both from education and experience. He stresses the essential truth that entrepreneurship is opportunism, which means not just recognising one of the thousands of opportunities available, but seizing the chosen chance by the throat. He provides invaluable advice on how to combine risk-taking (the essence of entrepreneurship) with prudence (the essential virtue of business).

As a great Asian thinker once put it, "Never let an opportunity pass by, but always think twice before acting". The advice is self-evidently sound, but there's a catch. What's the difference between the entrepreneur and the manager? When Forbat recommends TASK – the acronym from Think, Analyse, Solve and Kill [the problem] – what is he preaching that a good manager in any sizeable company shouldn't practise? And don't all managers also require his four T's: Truth, Tact, Thick skin and Toughness? In answering his own question – what is an entrepreneur? – Forbat lists five attributes which are plainly invaluable to any business manager. He or (increasingly) she is:

1 An indefatigable visionary with a clear goal.

2 A (measured) risk-taker.

3 Willing to push the boundaries to develop markets.

4 Persistent but patient and determined to succeed.

5 A professional manager and a good communicator.

The difference is that the corpocrat can get by with only some, or even none, of the five attributes. The entrepreneur cannot, for he stakes his career and often his economic survival on winning a successful outcome. Striking out (by definition) on new ground, he has nothing on which to fall back – no corporate history, no established organisation. The dead weight of history and establishment, however, is a prime reason for the much-lamented (and unnecessary) inability of large corporations to create the entrepreneurial cadres and businesses to which they pay so much lip service.

This doesn't mean that entrepreneurs are born, and can never be made. Given the right conditions, unlikely people can become thrusting opportunists. Forbat makes a brilliant example of turnarounds, where he has much experience. In case after case, failing companies, with much the same management but different leadership, have been moved in double-quick time from 'insolvency' to 'takeover target'; or, if you prefer, basket case to boomlet.

One of Forbat's case studies lists no less than 25 turnaround requirements, from the necessity of giving the chief executive or managing director "full authority and freedom… for the speedy measures required" to insistence on "zero company politics and on full communication – up/down and laterally". As he says, "with total dedication, persistence and stamina, it is possible to dig a failing company out of the deepest hole". The 25 recommendations, reminded me irresistibly of the following list, drawn from the turnaround of ICI by Sir John Harvey-Jones:

1 Leadership is the fulcrum.

2 Nothing is sacred.

3 Decisions are taken firmly when and where they must be taken.

4 Action is taken equally decisively.

5 What is being done, when and with what results must be clearly communicated inside and outside the firm.

6 Change must be facilitated and strongly symbolised by unmistakeable actions.

7 The basics of the business must be got and kept right.

8 The future lies ahead.

Two powerful thoughts arise from this list of the decisive (le mot juste) characteristics of turnaround management. First, the same generalisation applies: they are principles of all effective management in all circumstance. Second, the last of the octet is critical, and the one that separates the entrepreneur from the corpocrat. The latter often lives in the past: the former makes the future happen. The corpocrat lives and rules by old statistics, overwhelmingly by financial measures: the entrepreneur knows that "success cannot be measured by the accounting figures alone".

Forbat goes on to ask: "Is the company creating the conditions for future success?" There is no more important question. A dusty answer explains why so many terrific turnarounds go into reverse (as happened, disastrously, with ICI), the turnaround manager focuses too exclusively on the pressures of the present and forgets about what happens next. This Achilles heel is the mirror image of the entrepreneur's notorious weakness: racing towards the future, but not getting the present basics right.

That's when 'professional management' is often brought in, often with unhappy results as the imported pro clashes hopelessly with the entrenched entrepreneur. Anybody who follows Forbat's teaching on people management will avoid this trap. He believes in turning employees, from the top to the bottom, into allies, rightly arguing that "If employees are treated with equal respect and consideration, their loyalty follows" and that "when necessity for 'unreasonable' efforts is candidly explained, employees behave like entrepreneurs".

Note the word 'unreasonable'. The reasonable nature of entrepreneurial ambitions often appears only in hindsight. Was it reasonable for a young geek in Seattle to foresee and work for a time (not far away) when every desk would support a personal computer, using Microsoft programs? Was it reasonable for a veteran retailer in Benton, Ohio to embark on a town-by-town expansion that made Wal-Mart the world's greatest retailer? You could almost define entrepreneurship as the pursuit of unreasonable ambitions by reasonable means.

Forbat is equally instructive on the ends and the means, and on both starting up and cashing in. In a business world where the pace of change has become quite frightening, the entrepreneur must still run faster than everybody else. There is, of course, one consolation. He or she can also hope to outdo everybody else in creating wealth – most notably for themselves.

Robert Heller

1

WHAT IS AN ENTREPRENEUR?

What Is An Entrepreneur?

Everybody would like to make money and unless one starts with a silver spoon that happens to be already in place, success will usually depend on the degree of enterprise that is intelligently applied to the business idea. Many well-landed inheritors of wealth have finished up penniless despite their favourable start, because they lack either enterprise or professionalism, or both. Or they may not be hungry enough! Necessity can be a real mother of invention.

Whether it is the latest "dot.com" idea or carving reproduction antique furniture, there has to be a vision and it has to be related to a credible market. The market may not be self evident to everybody (especially to bankers and other sources of venture funds), and it may not be greatly evident to the targeted buyers of the vision, but it has to be clear enough to become credible in the real world of the target market. There will be obstacles galore, from unbelieving finance houses to sceptical buyers, but the entrepreneur with the vision and understanding of the market will not be easily deterred.

Assuming all this, alone or with others he will be a canny risk taker – not just an optimistic dreamer, but a determined realist. Be it financial, technical or operational, his risk taking will always be measured and remain within his resources, yet all the time he can see his objective remains credible, he will pursue his stony path with dogged persistence and generally won't take "No" for an answer. Sometimes this means going against conventional wisdom and the advice of experts. Seeking, evaluating and considering advice will be part of the risk assessment, but when the chips are down, since only he will be deeply involved enough in the details, nobody else can take the responsibility or the decisions. If he already has enough business experience, professional research and evaluation have to combine with the entrepreneur's gut feeling and he will usually be right to trust his instincts.

Overcoming obstacles and inertia in others will require the entrepreneur to exercise patience as well as persistence. Prospective customers always have to be found, tracked down while in motion, addressed and persuaded. When the entrepreneur is starting without an acknowledged track record in his chosen market, motivation, determination and persistence can be more important than brilliance.

No faint hearts in entrepreneurship at age 16 learning to fly solo from first flight.

No faint hearts will succeed, since few entrepreneurs have found easy pickings without putting in the necessary effort. Besides constant attention to detail and analysis of the ever-changing situation, this can mean working harder than almost any employee and being able and willing to go on and on until the job is done. His very waking hours and sometimes his sleeping hours will be engaged on his vision. This requires stamina and the confidence to take a necessary break at the right time – perhaps with his mobile phone and his laptop within easy reach.

Overlaid upon these personal traits, the entrepreneur has to have integrity. It sounds trite, but it shows through in behaviour and is soon perceived by customers and collaborators alike. Bringing natural respect and loyalty, the prospects for success of an enterprise is immeasurably enhanced when integrity is seen to emanate from its pores.

There are no guarantees in life, but entrepreneurs with the necessary traits are likely to make serious money – even if this requires a number of years. Most American millionaires have built their business from small beginnings over many years and finally sold out for their happy retirement in the sun.

What is it like, to be a one-man band entrepreneur? On a bad day in America it could start like this:

"Now, what have I forgotten? Perhaps nothing, but I must be on the way to the airport by four to beat the traffic. Let's just check – the customer file has all the correspondence and a copy of the contract – I mustn't risk losing that contract, my only copy, yet I may not need it on this trip. No, there isn't time to remove it from the very bottom of the file and where should I file it anyway, just for a couple of days? No point in opening a new file – I suppose it would have to go under 'T' for 'temporary' or for 'trips'. I shall never remember that by Wednesday and then I'll be hunting for it. Nothing more frustrating than looking for something in a great hurry, when you can almost put your hand on it but somehow it escapes and then the telephone rings. Ah, it must be..... then the first ring removes all traces of memory.

Damn! There IS the phone. If only the 'Executive Suite' receptionist could get to know something about my main clients, she might know when to take a message and when to interrupt me. I suppose it takes a good private secretary a few months, so how can I expect her to know? 'Call from New York.' 'Yes, this is he; what? Five hundred pens with my choice of advertising message, for $250 and win a free Jacuzzi; no thank you!' Now, where was I?

Yes, remember the draft agency agreement, the technical brochures and the price sheets. How long do I have? It's one o'clock and now everybody in the office suite has gone for lunch, but nobody thought to check whether I need anything brought in. I'll never last till that airline dinner – I'll jump in the car and run down to the sandwich shop for a tuna salad on rye. Must deposit those cheques on the way. Can't have the account too bare. Isn't the rent due this week? I bet the accountant will call with a list of things as long as my arm, of expenditures to be allocated between overhead and job costs. All itsy bitsy details he must have before he can complete the financial statement, I thought I had already marked them on the invoices. Perhaps I can get away first, then we can put it off till I return from Minneapolis.

Yes, until I can justify an assistant who can let me get on with the real work, I shall definitely type my own correspondence. Thank heavens for personal computers. It will definitely save the overhead and make me really appreciate how easy life used to be, when I could concentrate on the business in hand and leave the office routine to others. My next secretary will have a most enlightened and appreciative boss, I swear!

Makes me weep almost, another job application from a young marketing graduate. I had two from thirty-year old MBAs last month. Hell! How I could use one of those chaps. But there is no way. Until a couple more customers make a real commitment and budget accordingly, $40,000 for an inexperienced graduate is out of the question. As for the MBAs, the last one was looking for $75,000. That super executive secretary I interviewed last year could have been a great help with the desk research as well as the routine, but she was already making $27,000 plus the usual benefits.

Sooner or later, I shall be able to consider a serious prospect. Perhaps a keen young graduate intern, who is willing to learn about the real meaning of entrepreneurship the hard way. If he is too proud to lick stamps, or to make thirty telephone calls in an afternoon, chasing unwilling, unavailable company presidents, well I'm not, so let him go to a Fortune 500 company and be a small cog in their vast machine.

Gosh, all this dreaming in the sandwich shop and post office lines – I have one hour before racing to the airport. No less than six telephone messages, none of them from those people I have been calling without success. Why won't people return calls? By Murphy's Law, any long distance enquiries come only while I am out of the office, leaving me to make and to pay for the several response calls inevitably needed before we actually connect. With some reliable staff, instead of finding merely a message with a name and telephone number on my desk, I might find an intelligent report, giving details of the company, their products and their market aspirations, even sensible follow up arrangements, already in train.

Time to leave. Throw the garment bag into the trunk, with briefcase full of papers and a coat for Northern climates. Why am I always bathed in sweat, when I reach my seat? Two hours is barely enough to dry out and brush up the appearance before meeting another new face.

I must use the time we are not eating to read the host company's profile and product literature. Yet, I have never known such absolute freedom. So long as I can keep the clients satisfied, nobody can prevent me from coming and going as and when I please. There are no holiday lists, no priority travel arrangements, no P's and Q's to be watched. If I should take a trip, leave early or late, extend my visit to England by three weeks, bring my wife to the party etc., etc., nobody but nobody can disagree with me. I just need somebody to make sure that I remember to stuff the enclosures into the correct letter before I seal it down. It makes such a mess when they are reopened!

Wake up! Dreaming again, let's get down to reading that contract and product literature. We shall be landing in twenty minutes."

Before the reader is completely put off and decides against becoming an entrepreneur, it should be said that most days start off less stressfully and under better control. It is almost a relief to know, that there is nobody to screw things up but yourself! And you have absolute freedom – to sink or swim.

In summary, an entrepreneur is:

- An indefatigable visionary with a clear goal.
- A (measured) risk taker.
- Willing to push the boundaries to develop markets.
- Persistent but patient and determined to succeed.
- A professional manager and a good communicator.

2

APPRENTICESHIP BEFORE ENTREPRENEURSHIP

Apprenticeship Before Entrepreneurship

For those with natural acumen or immersed in a family business environment from an early age, the garage or kitchen start up, with or without a convenient pot of gold, may lead to success. Bill Gates, Philip Green and Alan Sugar did it but one can generally count such success stories on the fingers of one hand. Before embarking on an entrepreneurial adventure, it is usually best to get some solid experience in the business world.

Even business schools do not teach many of the lessons discussed in this chapter. If you have gone through college, where life is relatively predictable and structured, there is something to be said for starting one's business career in an established company – where it is difficult not to learn from others' mistakes. Nevertheless, large corporations can be bureaucratic, making life within them constrained and dependent on others for day-to-day decisions. The smaller the company, or the more enlightened and capable its management, the greater scope will there be to exercise initiative. In small companies, there need never be a shortage of challenges and there is plenty of stimulation and pressure to keep the adrenalin flowing.

One would expect versatility – essential for entrepreneurship – to come with experience, but it is also a matter of mental attitude. So what are the important principles for a young person to follow, on entering the competitive world of industry or commerce?

Firstly, work at something you enjoy and become proficient at it. It is no good starting off as a wide looking generalist, who knows little about anything. Very few people can start off as King and work up from there! Your sights must initially be concentrated on becoming professionally educated and then well practiced in a chosen vocation. This will enable you to do your particular job well, to earn the respect of those around and above, and it will provide a springboard for greater things.

The next thing is to do a lot of listening. A university degree mainly enables one to realise how much more there is to know. Without listening, you will learn very little and the most important things to learn are not so much the technicalities of the work, but how it is organised in the company and who is and does what and why.

Then think. Always think, work out why, figure out solutions to problems, then suggest, recommend and help to make decisions. The latter is not always popular with those who have been there for years. They may well argue all the reasons against your fresh ideas. Yet their objections may be based on good experience, not just pique, so listen and remember how little you really know. Your ideas are probably good and with listening, they will get better. By using tact and good psychology, your ideas will gradually be accepted.

Obviously, you must please your boss. Not by flattery or by bringing flowers, but by doing your job better than he ever imagined and by doing it intelligently, which means effectively and efficiently. Any boss worth his salt likes to see his juniors work out their own problems, take into account peripheral (other people's) problems and to finish ahead of time, well inside budget. If you see something needs doing, which your boss did not ask for, then do it as a bonus, first making sure that this does not encroach on others' work and cause unnecessary difficulties. All this makes it easier for your boss to do his job and he may even mention your stalwart efforts to his boss. I always recall my first boss's amazement when I asked for my next task, on completing one, just five minutes before finishing time. It was enthusiasm and impatience, not play-acting and he could see it. He became my best supporter and fought for my raises each year end.

However much you need and wish to prove yourself, even in the smallest of companies, it is teamwork which determines success or failure. Prima donnas are out of place and can cause much strife, completely negating their talents.

Another essential principle to success is that every problem has a solution. There must be no "impossibles" which cannot be resolved by proper application of thought and perseverance. When faced with a smooth high wall and the need to reach the other side, for commandos it must always be possible to succeed somehow. How high? How thick? What is on the other side? How can we co-operate to get each other over? What equipment can we use? Can we go around it to the East or the West? It is management's job to provide the necessary resources and if these are inadequate for the job in hand, the needs must be spelled out, whether they are people, material or finance. It is only necessary to think, to analyse, to solve and then to kill the problem.

- **T**HINK
- **A**NALYSE
- **S**OLVE
- **K**ILL

TASK is the principle to follow if you want to ensure success of a project or a business.

Returning to the subject of teamwork, it is easy to oversimplify this to equal delegation. This is vital of course; each team member being delegated clearly defined tasks, which the team manager co-ordinates and welds into a unified effort. But teamwork is only possible if there is loyalty, and loyalty is required in all directions; upward loyalty to the boss, loyalty to others in the team and loyalty from above. Any worthwhile manager will be as loyal to you and will fight for your benefit in the company, as you should be to him.

Loyalty permits criticism, but this must always be constructive. If you make a rule never to criticise a colleague's work without offering a credible alternative, you will not go far wrong. No reasonable person can take offence at constructive criticism.

Destructive criticism is an easy trap for those mainly concerned with scoring points over others. It leads to company politics – the worst scourge of any group. It destroys teamwork and co-operation and can occupy a dominant part of people's time and thought at the expense of the business and all those in it. In large companies, politics can take over the lives of middle managers and reach the top. Like a cancer, it is difficult to fight or to eliminate. As a good "servant" of your boss, it can be only too easy to become embroiled, but don't!

There are always escape routes, which can prevent you becoming part of this syndrome. Although it may appear advantageous to get onto the right (or the boss's) side, those who stay out of company politics and are seen to remain objective will build a reputation for integrity which will stand them in good stead. If you happen to land in a company where politics appears to be inescapable it may be better to look elsewhere.

Politics can only really be scotched from the very top and this requires the chief executive to know it goes on and he must have the desire and the will to put a stop to it. At all levels, including the "freshman", the best way to keep clean is to be open about everything. If you disagree with somebody, say so with well thought out reasons and be prepared to be convinced otherwise. Tact may sometimes dictate that you do not express your disagreement in public but instead leave it to the earliest private opportunity. If you are told to do something which you think is stupid, loyalty to the boss requires you to carry it out, but loyalty to the company and to yourself requires you to state the argument as you see it, openly and without malice, sarcasm or sniping.

Equally true in all business dealings, the answer to politics and to most relationships could be summarised by the four T's:

- **T**RUTH
- **T**ACT
- **T**HICK SKIN
- **T**OUGHNESS

Remember, nobody is indispensable!

When preparing for life as an entrepreneur, ambition is a good trait and within the restraints just discussed, so you should not be afraid of it. To further your career, you must know your job better than anybody else and you must constantly strive to see the big picture surrounding your function. This will enable you to do your own job better, but if you know how it affects other people, departments and the whole company, your usefulness will multiply and incidentally, you will derive more satisfaction from your job.

You must learn and understand the objectives of your company and the effect of your personal efforts on their achievement. A junior lab assistant or young salesman will have an influence on his company, despite the many other more experienced people around. What is more, if you look at how you could exert more (constructive) influence in the way you do your job, you will be actively identifying with the company's needs and objectives. That is what will lift you from the crowd of "ordinary guys" and give you visibility with management and with its customers. Remember also, that bad relationships lead to poor profits.

As entrepreneur or employee, your function is to fulfil, as close to 100% as possible, the demands of the company's customers and the nature and problems of the customers' business must be clearly understood.

A profit and loss account or a balance sheet is not difficult to understand, but their appreciation and analysis are key to running a business. As a future entrepreneur, always see yourself as a part of the whole; learn how the company operates throughout its organisation and how it relates to the outside world. How are its products sold? Who are its customers and what are their problems? Who provides the finances – private shareholders, the stock market – or the immediate margins on sales, which depend on how much you cost the company? Understand the finer points of costing, gross and net profit margins, which are of course of primary importance however the company is financed, but their inadequacy can be quickly fatal if there are no other funds to draw upon. Above all in accounting, understand the control of cash flow and how this can be optimised by negotiating favourable terms of trade. Seemingly high profits and margins must always come under suspicion if cash flow is leaving the bank account empty.

Can you identify with the objectives of the board of directors and do you know the level of risk being taken by the shareholders? These are all matters of importance to anybody with ambition when entering the business world from the first day. Their importance requires him to keep on learning about his own job, about marketing, economics, finance – that is about business as a whole, in order to see the big picture.

Equally necessary to the entrepreneur, man management is the art of maintaining an effective balance between positive leadership and delegation. The first requirement is that of good communication. Vital in selling and in negotiating, this involves information being transmitted, it being intelligent, properly received and fully understood. Otherwise, communication has failed and nothing useful will have been imparted.

There is a story of the motorist who lost his way and stopped at a garage, to ask for directions. A neat intelligent looking man with a briefcase was passing and the motorist asked, "Can you tell me where this is?" Without hesitation, the man answered, "You are outside a Texaco station, twenty five yards from a stop sign". Being quick to grasp situations, the motorist asked, "Are you an accountant?" to which the surprised man said "Yes, but how did you guess?" "Very simple," said the motorist, "You gave me a piece of information which is 100% accurate, but absolutely useless!" Fortunately, this is not true of all accountants, but it is all too easy to ignore the purpose of information. Furthermore, it is the duty of the possessor of information to pass it to those who need it. It is no use telling a sinking man that he did not ask you whether there was quicksand in his path. It is your responsibility to recognise a situation in the light of your knowledge and to impart any information to those who may need it.

Secondly, motivation is necessary for all man management and it is well to remember that everybody – particularly a customer or client – likes his ideas to be solicited, seriously considered, acted upon and his interests protected. It is natural to desire the feeling of being wanted and appreciated.

Within a company or relating to a client looking for a win-win situation, successful man (or customer) management requires the recognition of common goals. This requires the clear definition of every need and prospective solution. The relationships with those one wishes to manage must never be cosmetic, but genuine, which means you must really care about them and about the other party's interests.

Finally, there is the question of respect. This can only be earned and requires the demonstration of professionalism, work dedication, consistency of actions and attitudes, as well as fairness. Whether it is the boss or the customer, you need to earn respect and there is no better way than by example.

With such principles, you can embark on running your own business without being daunted, but excited by the prospect. Just remain creative, tough and willing to take your own risks.

In summary:

- Get a good education.
- Become proficient in a trade or occupation that you enjoy.
- Immerse yourself in the business of a company and see the big picture.
- Learn to analyse business situations in the widest sense.
- TASK: Think – Analyse – Solve – Kill the problem.
- The four Ts: Truth – Tact – Thick skin – Toughness.
- Listen, prepare to quantify and to take risk.
- Be decisive.

3

JUMPING ON OPPORTUNITIES

Jumping On Opportunities

The entrepreneur will start with perhaps £100; the designer may start with the proverbial blank sheet of paper. Both may have a vision, an insatiable desire to see an idea come true. In the entrepreneur's case the vision often coincides with an opportunity waiting to be seized. Alternatively, an opportunity is created by sheer persistence. Of course, there may be an immense gulf between the ultimate reality and the much more common, and usually unrealised, hope. That is why, although luck will play a part in the success of an entrepreneur, skills in preferably several of the professional disciplines tend to separate the lasting successes from the bankruptcy cases.

The first requirement is to recognise an opportunity, then to grasp it. The process could be likened to that of a free rider standing by a railway track as trains of all sizes and speeds go by, inviting a decision to jump. Once past, the right train may not come by again. It needs to be going in the right direction. If it's not going too fast, the rider can always jump off before his situation becomes too precarious. Unstable tracks will give advance warning of the need to slow down, or stop, or jump off. With sufficient foresight and intelligence, it may even be possible to switch trains, or alter direction by judicious application to the signals and points. But if the tracks run out into barren country, or among savages (and these cannot always be seen from an earlier jumping off point), the journey could end disastrously.

I once designed a product, carried out some market research, and produced a detailed business plan which arrested the attention of virtually every significant potential market outlet in the business. It was a maternity belt, originally constructed for my wife who wore it during her fifth pregnancy until the last minute. It made all the difference to her comfort. While other products all caused discomfort and were generally discarded when most needed, my product did not merely do the job, but it could be sold at about half the price and still provide its maker with a return on capital of over 50% within a reasonable time of launching.

Since this was in a marketing area in which I was inexperienced, and where the proper outlets had to be available, I approached the corset manufacturers and the maternity retail chains, which all gave the project serious consideration. In the end, they all shied away. Perhaps they did not have the courage to try a new line. Perhaps they wanted to protect their existing designs. From a lack of capital, or the patience to see the project through the slow way, by building my own production and gradually worming my way into the market, I lost an opportunity. The trade also lost an opportunity and a comparable product has only come onto the market some forty years later!

In this instance, I had neither the production nor selling capabilities to carry the project through on my own. If one of these facilities is available, it is sometimes possible to find a partner with the complementary know-how. When a business opportunity is big enough to require the risking of real money, one or both of the partners require sufficient courage and confidence in the project to take that deep breath and to dive in. (This leads to the question of market research, of which more later.) Many an entrepreneur has mortgaged his house, perhaps for the second time, to obtain the funds for starting up on his own. If it is necessary to rely on the commitment of effort and cash from another company, it can be extremely difficult to change priorities. It requires special motivation to go for a new project at all, when existing products are supporting the business. Plus, motivation is least easy to sustain in big businesses, where perhaps ten people, at three levels of management, may need to be in accord before a new course of action can be approved.

Perhaps the greatest mother of entrepreneurship, as of invention, is necessity. When a business is visibly declining or a prime product is obsolescent, or on a personal level, when somebody has resigned or has been made redundant, under these circumstances, a decision to take a risk is the lesser of two evils, even for the cautious. For example, the price war in the personal computer business caused numerous redundancies. It also provided the stimulus for at least one area sales manager to set up as an independent dealer on behalf of several manufacturers, including his previous employers. His was a lonely and hard life, but his overheads were mainly in his dining room. The leisure goods business is another fast train onto which some people have made a timely jump, particularly in areas where there are few retail outlets, to meet a growing demand for sports goods. The margins are high and it is possible to obtain regular bulk orders from clubs to offset the high stock requirements of the shop.

It is always worth pursuing the opportunity that arises when a large company wishes to replace an obsolescent line with something within a small company's expertise. For instance, a company which manufactures several million hypodermic needles per week would be vulnerable to the replacement of conventional injection techniques by a pressure jet. It may therefore need to introduce a new product quickly, and be happy to subcontract components. Unlike the maternity belt, the new product could be a salvation rather than a risk.

Marketing text books rightly say that a business has to provide something for which there is a real demand: Hence the need for proper market research. But in a small business, the problem needs an approach different from that in a big business. The principles of market research are, of course, constant and the practice is always to ask the market what it wants. It is essential to avoid answers which do not reflect real desires, so the questions must not be loaded to any particular end. Indeed, the value of a market research report depends most of all on the skill applied to framing the questions. Thus, "Would you prefer your four-cylinder, five-seater independent front-suspension sports coupe to be red, green or mustard?" may provide an unambiguous answer. It will not tell you if the interviewee prefers to travel by bus. On the other hand, to ask whether "A high-density rapid-transit transportation system would suit your commuting needs" may lead to answers totally dependent on the interpretation in the mind of the researcher who could finish up getting the answers he really hopes to hear. The more open, objective and unbiased the research, the more likely is the marketer to arrive at the saleable specification.

However, full-scale market research projects are frequently costed in many thousands of pounds. This could be entirely justified for the big business, when the result may lead to the commitment of hundreds of thousands or even millions to development, tooling, production and sales promotion. Such projects take time to specify, longer to carry out and a further period to analyse. The whole cycle could easily take more than six months, and the cost incurred internally could well equal the amount spent outside on the market research contract. At the end of the whole procedure, the answer may be a lemon. The train may also have gone by in the meantime.

Close personal contact with customers

A small business can rarely go through such a complete and professional process for lack of both funds and time. However, an entrepreneur worth his salt will be in close personal contact with his market. He must be careful to distinguish between what he learns about market needs and his own desires and he must face facts squarely if they don't match what he wants to hear. He and his small sales team should seek and analyse market data on a continuous basis. With the appropriate effort before making product changes and similar decisions, a set of market data will be obtained which may lack some of the breadth of the professional survey but which will be like a rapier thrust, in much greater depth. A small business may thus be able to obtain its market data to a sufficiently accurate level at no extra expense and in reasonable time. It may be able to channel funds to capital expenditure or R&D instead, at least up to the feasibility and market testing stages.

When the market itself comes to the small business, which has become known for its expertise in a given field, the need for market research may totally disappear. Such an approach is by no means rare, and can come from an organization having all the outlets that are so time-consuming and expensive to build up and which is in a position to carry out painstaking market research. Of course, the small company might not get the job, for all the established big company reasons. However, the small man will have had the chance to inspect a fair-sized train while in motion, whether it distributes hypodermic needles to hospitals or accessories to the garage trade.

The small business is also in a position to justify 'opportunity marketing' whenever a small opportunity comes along. In this case, the need can often be met from existing know-how, and from existing product or service capabilities. A small but positive effort at supplying an immediate service may keep the wolf from the door, even if it may not suggest the need for a five-year plan. As long as the activity is profitable from the start, and it fits in with the capabilities and general objectives of the business, it can be worthwhile boarding this slow train. Larger businesses often consider such small beer unworthy of their attention, and clearly have to beware of dissipating effort over too many small projects. Nevertheless, the marginal gross profit may well greatly outweigh the marginal increase in management effort, which in a small business is frequently that of the entrepreneur himself and easily within his reach.

Even in big business, however, there may be a place for opportunity marketing. The purpose may not be to create something from nothing, but to preserve something, which would otherwise rapidly become nothing. A major aircraft and weapons company operated a capable department equipped for the environmental testing of weapon prototypes. The department had facilities for heating, freezing, humidifying, vibrating, and for choking test samples with dust and salt spray. But when the weapons contracts thinned out there was redundancy among the laboratory staff. At first the company was not willing to heed proposals to seek test work from other organizations, even though this would keep a good team together and utilise valuable capital plant. However, within a year or two, pride and fixed attitudes gave way to necessity, and to a form of opportunity marketing and a steady business in subcontract test services.

Of course, opportunity marketing has a dubious claim to the name of marketing, but there are always a few brave souls willing to turn marketing logic upside down, and to tell the market what it needs. Such arrogance is generally, though not always, characteristic of small entrepreneurs. The cure for which there is no ill does not deserve to be sold and the small business entrepreneur who conscientiously exercises his judgment will not fall into this trap. But the absence of positive research findings doesn't necessarily mean there is no market. How many people, for example, demanded to wear seatbelts in cars? It needed legislation to compel car manufacturers to fit them and, after that, it required yet further legislation to make car occupants wear them. Yet some arrogant entrepreneurs set out to convince the market that it needed seatbelts – and finished up in big business. This type of marketing, if successful, really is creating something from nothing. It requires enormous perseverance and patience and provides more than ample opportunity to make mistakes, but it can also lead to a golden period of lone leadership in the market – until the wolves of competition catch up. Success in creating a market, particularly among big business customers, is sweet indeed.

Case studies in creating unrecognised markets

Safety features

Intrinsically, trying to sell a safety feature to car manufacturers is rather like persuading elderly Anglo-Saxon housewives to campaign in favour of the metric system. The thing has an obvious and logical future, but life would be so much easier if it went away. In the motor industry, even in good times, it could require a full-scale board meeting to consider the addition of just a 5p item to the specification. Safety features, which did not visibly add to the line, decor or performance of the product tended to rate a very low priority. Yet, as an entrepreneur, I argued that in the long run, a truly valid safety feature must eventually sell. Market influences in such a case are much more complex than either the motorist or the manufacturer. They may include among others, government departments and their laboratories, distribution chains, retail and service outlets, even international committees; acceptance of the product may turn on the support of several of these organizations. This alone makes any decision improbable. Under the circumstances it might appear true arrogance for a small business to attempt the creation of something new in the automotive market. Yet my company did just this on an international scale. It started with a fundamentally excellent technical concept, a clear realization of potential uses, and fully documented knowledge of the relevant accident statistics and casualty rates.

These essentials were coupled to painstaking product engineering, with a keen eye on costs to achieve an acceptable price. While my company was surviving largely on opportunity markets, acceptance of the car safety product gradually built up. The first production order was taken on a profitable basis, but required concurrent investment in relatively expensive tooling and continuing engineering effort. Effective effort at the marketing end was basically limited to my chief executive level part-time attention in working hours, and a lot more research and thinking time in the bath. There was, in addition, the equivalent of one full-time person for design, testing and production engineering.

Within a few years, a small part of the potential market was generating a turnover well into six figures (at 1970s values), regular shipments were being made to three countries, and a major international car manufacturer had paid a substantial fee for licence rights. Further test programmes were in hand with nearly every major car company in the world, and the first stages of safety legislation requiring such products had been announced, but the early, faltering steps toward success took four or five years to reach a fast walk. We gained a large part of our market knowledge as we went along; while I battled away at all levels, from board directors to junior test engineers, in motor companies all over Europe, in Detroit, and in Tokyo. By staying the course, engaging in the most professional engineering and quality assurance and manufacturing down to a price, the cure for which there is no ill sold profitably worldwide, multiplying turnover until the company's shares were listed on the London Stock Exchange.

Electronic security

Among the opportunity products we tackled, one, apparently unrelated to our then current line, became the heart of its business. The company turned to an entirely new market but in doing so, it came up against the practices and attitudes of many years, so that enormous persistence was needed to create something from the germ of a favourable reaction. The industry related to security systems and had built up a considerable resistance to any new technique since so many had cost it dearly in the past. Our company appeared to be offering a product employing the same principle as earlier products, which caused nothing but false alarms. What was more, the product offered protection on the perimeters of buildings – where false alarms seemed most likely – so adding to the scepticism of those who had been in the business for twenty years and knew it all. However, since the product was truly capable of dealing with problems which the industry had come to regard as hopeless, the company knew there really was a market need.

To get its product on the market, the company needed to obtain close familiarity with the detailed problems of security installations and to undertake careful and imaginative applications engineering. Then it had to run detailed tests, and give patient demonstrations to the security and insurance industries. It just refused to give up and had to develop speedy reactions to compensate for the inevitable mistakes of one who is new to a market. The selling effort, which doubled this business annually and soon reached well into six figures, came essentially from one full-time man and up to half my time at chief executive level. Yet the business became established in the US and Canada, across most of Western Europe and in Australia, with embryonic operations in the Middle East and South Africa. High on the list of reasons for the company's success was the willingness to put consistent development effort into the product, into its quality and into after-sales service. The creative process also called for the motivation of distributors, who had to be found, convinced, trained – and then repeatedly prodded.

These examples run counter to some of the conventional principles of marketing. However, they do illustrate the way in which innovative success can be a function of the entrepreneurial small business environment. The opportunity to create something from nothing can be seized by recognizing a special kind of synergy. This is a compatibility between something which the company is already doing and that which it could do without needing to persuade a distant, cautious and unbelieving corporate headquarters. It has to be added that some of the most successful big businesses in the US and in the UK have been those which made a habit of creating and fostering small divisions. They were generally allowed to run as virtually independent businesses under the control of managers with wide powers to develop their ideas, and the opportunity to reap benefits normally available only to successful entrepreneurs.

A modern business may develop along either market, or production-oriented paths, as long as there is sufficient synergy to keep risk and expenditure down to acceptable levels. A small business must be wary of entering new markets that demand a distribution complex which is too broad for it to handle. It must be shy of products requiring technical know-how or production facilities which are too far removed from those already available and equally cautious about techniques unfamiliar to its people. However, it is frequently possible to fill a recognized technical gap by employing consultants, universities or research organizations, or, best of all, by recruiting someone with the required skills into the business.

A satisfying habit of coming back

Having established a claim to a skill which is not freely available elsewhere, the entrepreneur will find that the market has a satisfying habit of coming back to him with its requirements. These may seem wondrous until seen to be compatible with the capabilities of the business. The case of my company, which became known for its expertise in the detection of small shocks and vibrations in building structures – without confusing these with normal environmental movements – is a ready example. In a totally different market area, it was approached to provide a means of detecting the approach of high-speed trains, one more convenient and efficient than that provided by mechanically contacting treadles which require regular replacement. It was also offered the opportunity to devise a means of detecting earthquakes in Japan so that gas supplies to buildings might be shut off before any fires started. These needs may appear unrelated and remote from the company's markets, but they have synergy in that they promise to adapt technology which is well established in the firm.

The cases of the railways and the earthquakes are themselves entirely different. The railways represent a single (if complex) customer who can be serviced by one person in the early days. If the venture succeeds, a sales approach to foreign railways will be well justified. The earthquake problem is a little distant from Britain, but if the requirement comes from a single source which will look after distribution, a few visits to Japan will be more than worthwhile. There will be a need for regular attention and follow-up during the early days of developing a project at such great distance. This, together with the after-sales effort which will be needed by the distant distributor at least until he has a trained support team himself, must be remembered and budgeted for.

The questions are:

- How big is the market?
- Do our know-how and private-venture budget extend to the first step of investigation?
- Indeed, can the remaining steps towards fruition of the project be chosen so as to keep costs compatible with the progress and apparent potential of the project?
- In maximizing the opportunities presented by a market, what are the risks of relying on others to develop the market at a great distance?

Perhaps the biggest risk is to assume that market development will proceed in the same manner and with the same priority as if it were being carried out in the company's own territory. However well placed and well qualified an overseas partner, it is still necessary to pay close attention to the marketing end. In a small business, this almost inevitably means working alongside a distributor, agent or licensee.

Each partner wishes to minimise risk. For the overseas agent, this takes the form of requiring exclusivity for as long a period as possible. Back home, the entrepreneur will want the maximum range of options, with power to fire the agent if he does not perform. At the same time he needs to offer sufficient incentive for the agent to put energetic and sustained effort into the business. Similarly, with prices. When placing an uncertain product into a new market, the businessman will try to cover his risks by asking the highest possible price. The agent will want the lowest price and the highest mark-up to cover his selling costs – and might well reach for prices which the market is reluctant to pay. He may want to spread the risk further – or make up for insufficient capability – by working through an additional level of dealer. This could further increase prices in the market, or depress the required level of factory prices. Thus the entrepreneur must remain personally involved with a market even when it is nominally being handled by a more competent local partner. He must have close familiarity with its conditions and limitations in order to be able to argue his case effectively.

Reasonable compromise is usual

Reasonable compromise usually prevails in the end. It is rare to get an ideal deal, let alone an ideal agent. Most will agree to a one-year trial period, during which it should be possible to begin penetrating the market and to see whether the business is going to grow, whether support for the agent is satisfactory from his point of view, whether a smooth business relationship and routine can be established. Some distribution organizations – particularly the big ones – soon lose heart if success does not come quickly. It is therefore essential to recognise the likely timescale of the initial sales build-up.

Agents are generally so worried about their costs that they demand two or more years of exclusive representation to ensure that they have time to recoup. All are afraid of being put out to grass if and when the business becomes worthwhile – which could earn the principal a deservedly bad reputation in the country concerned. (If a business is not going well – even if it's the agent's fault – he is usually only too glad to see it terminated.) All exclusive agreements should depend on performance measured by sales targets, and as long as corresponding safeguards are offered to the agent, by way of adequate renewal periods if targets are met, he should agree. The biggest difficulty usually comes at the start, when neither side knows what a realistic sales target might be. In this case, it might be possible to postpone agreement until the partners have six months' or a year's experience of working together.

Analogous questions apply on the product side. If an established product is regularly being distributed in a well-understood market, obviously it makes sense to add further products to the same channel, especially if this entails minimal increase in total selling costs. Many businessmen will prefer to protect their independence by developing their own products, and for major extensions of the business, this seems the logical way to go. However, a well-oiled sales network represents a whole series of opportunities. If trains go by which originate from different stations, and they can be directed to run along your length of track, it would be a pity not to jump on board. It might be possible to attract some opportunities your way by manufacturing under licence. This puts the boot firmly on the other foot if you are used to negotiating with distributors of your own products, but at least you should know the arguments. Here, the discussion comes back to market research and to the need for very careful evaluation.

Experience begets experience

Whether markets or products dominate the company's thinking, market know-how and product know-how feed on each other to the benefit of the business. Experience begets experience, contacts beget contacts. The entrepreneurial small business chief executive can still confine administration to a small part of his daily routine, so that he spends much of his time in contact with markets and products in their ever widening, intertwining development.

How far is it prudent to go in expanding a small business, to go on opening up new markets or developing new products? There is no single answer, of course, although there are a few commonsense rules. In the first place, there is probably a financial limitation. At every step of new endeavour it is essential to calculate the required effort, time and cost. If it is not certain that the project can be followed through without running out of funds or jeopardizing current business, don't jump onto the train. There is a limitation on management time, the chief executive's time and that of key sales and technical staff. In these cases, it is often possible to find a few extra hours, or outside help. Nevertheless, if shortage of time means you may launch a half-developed product or sell through the wrong channel, hesitate long enough to measure the deficiency. Never leap in the dark. An exception arises when there is clearly nothing to lose. Potentially, there may be a lot to be gained, as long as the proposition is reasonably well checked out.

It is sometimes possible to plan the direction of a development from the start, and to stick to the plan. More often, it is the seizing of opportunities in hands that can feel and with fingers which can mould which determines how the enterprise grows. As the creation process matures, the existing tends to constrain the projected, and a pattern will grow from it. The planning of an orderly future then becomes increasingly possible. The temptation to add further elements will be governed by powerful considerations of profitability, cash return to investors and the retention of entrepreneurial spirit in an established environment.

Some principles and lessons

- Keep a look out and don't miss a good looking opportunity – check it out quickly and act.
- Synergies with a company's existing products, or its markets, can justify new ventures.
- Market research can be more expensive than the cost of creating a product.
- The value of market research outcome is determined by the quality of the questions asked.
- Closely market-connected top management can often create the best market information.
- Opportunity marketing applies to big business, as well as to small companies.
- Case studies show that markets can be created where customers initially don't recognise a need – and can result in being without competition for some years.
- Markets come to the entrepreneurial company requesting them to supply a service.
- In distribution relationships, compromise becomes necessary between the supplier's price and ability to agree the distributor's margins and security of tenure.
- Check and calibrate all opportunities, but never leap in the dark.

4

AN ENTREPRENEURIAL EXTREME?

An Entrepreneurial Extreme?

Case study of an unlikely enterprise – operating on two continents, without capital

Not that most entrepreneurs would choose to embark on a project such as this one, however, dire necessity as a mother of enterprise can combine with the principle of jumping onto opportunities to create a possibly outlandish example of entrepreneurism. This real life personal case study will serve as an indication of how versatility, a willingness to move beyond past experience, to learn new things, and, above all, determination to overcome all obstacles by sheer application, persistence and stamina, can save bad situations and even bring rewards.

Beyond the age of 50 and left looking for the next step in an interrupted career, I received a call from a managing director in the security industry. His company manufactured access controls and needed a temporary solution to his problem in America: He had a new subsidiary and needed somebody with the necessary experience and track record to provide temporary management and then to hire a permanent manager to run it. "Would you like to discuss a three month assignment?" he asked.

It so happened that I had had a great deal of experience working with American companies and of exporting into the region, offering many contacts there. We negotiated a respectable monthly fee with reimbursed expenses, a rented, furnished "instant home" and a car in Atlanta with return flights to include my wife. The subsidiary had been set up in a decent office with a warehouse for selling, assembling, delivering and supporting access control systems. They needed responsible specifying, bidding and selling of projects, reliable project engineering, shipping and installation, with the usual service follow up and safeguards against technical problems and lawsuits. A little longer than anticipated, it took almost five months before I found and hired a new manager from Washington DC and he was ready to start at an organised operation in February. We returned to the UK for seven weeks to find out how and where I might continue a career, before going back to see the new man into the Atlanta company.

Close to my past experiences, I contemplated starting a permanent business in Atlanta, with similar fee-paid projects on behalf of European management wishing to enter the US market but lacking the required US based top management. Now having made many friends there, Georgia had decidedly got under our skin.

Leap into an uncertain future

Thus, after seeing the hired manager into the company I had put onto a sound footing, we decided to remain in Atlanta, perhaps to emigrate there. A Swedish company's need to license a product into the USA was under discussion and would have been an ideal continuation, with prospects in the sunny South. However, with return arrangements to Atlanta already set for just over a day's time, the licensing offer turned into a European sales job offer, but we declined it. Instead, we decided to continue with our travel arrangements without any firm business to take with us, only the expectation of finding similar European market entry clients to serve in America. Hope sprang eternal and now thoroughly committed, we took the leap.

Now we had no income whatsoever, only the remaining equity in the family home, emptied of progeny. Our bank had taken a charge on the house, and for living expenses I arranged a "brick by brick" monthly sub of $1,500 to be wired out to Atlanta. Of this, $800 was for the furnished instant home we continued to rent after our client's contract expired, leaving $700 a month for everything else, except for any necessary trips back to the UK. We kept my old company car, a Bentley which we had bought on my departure, and this was to be collected from Gatwick for shipping to the US – less expensive than buying a car there and valuable enough to provide a little insurance. Without any work awaiting me there, nor any contracts to take, this was truly a leap in the dark and my future appeared to be in the lap of the gods.

The car was not due to arrive for a couple of weeks, but true to Georgia hospitality, my past client's accountant not only agreed to lend us his spare car, he met us at the airport with the on loan Toyota and a large van for luggage. Neighbours we had known but for a few weeks came running from their houses in the Tahoe North development as we arrived. "Hi John and Mary, we missed you and we were worried in case you weren't coming back. Welcome home!" In the spare bedroom, the dining table extension-leaf was balanced on the TV plinth, bearing a telephone and the manual typewriter I had lugged from England. The chest of drawers was adapted as a filing cabinet. I spread out my blank sheet of paper and we were in business.

First office in Atlanta - starting from zero

The birth of IMEMCO

The first rudimentary prospectus sheets announcing International Market Entry Management Company (IMEMCO) soon followed, indicating "top management in place" to establish US operations for UK companies. My exporting experiences had made it abundantly clear that, however numerous, the typically two or three week long USA visits were never long enough to reach the people necessary for establishing business relationships, let alone making reasonably rapid progress toward getting sales or setting up distribution. The logic was simple enough; somebody with a successful record of business building and exporting at managing director level would know most of the vital questions – and many of the answers. If I was established in the US on a full time basis, I could apply myself, over a continuous term of months, make approaches and calls to the targeted people for as long as it took to track them down between their many meetings and travels. I would have time to press myself onto their generally distracted consciousness without being constrained by the time frame of a trip from a UK base, where the client's MD had many pressing priorities to demand his return. I could be the UK managing director's alter ego and work hand in glove with him according to an agreed set of objectives and programme of work, make instant local decisions and consensual major decisions as appropriate. The client MD could be brought over for well prepared and targeted visits of short duration, confident that he would be talking turkey rather than kicking his heels in hotel rooms while making fruitless telephone calls.

To win contracts, I would only need to work my many contacts on both sides of the Atlantic, find needy parties and propose suitable programmes of work. A reluctance to employ consultants remembered from my own years as an MD steered me towards presenting myself as a "make it happen" alter ego – like the client MD himself having his right hand living there in the US market. How could anybody wishing to enter the US market disagree?

Profitable pricing of this service had to recognize what is reasonable to pay in fees. Reckoning that my experience and past performance rated equally to senior partners in management consulting and accounting firms, I started with a daily rate taken at about half that charged by the major players with their high overheads. This came to $1,000 to $1,500 per day plus out of pocket telephone, fax and travel expenses. I knew this would scare the pants off any UK client, who would assume that I could work and charge 365 days per year. Realistically, I might be able to charge 100 days per year to cover office overheads and a living wage halfway comparable to US earning rates at this level. Avoiding the disclosure of this daily rate at all costs, I decided to make fixed price proposals based on time and travel estimates and explicit programmes of work over given numbers of weeks or months.

Looking for sources of referral and possible jointly worked projects, besides working my typewriter into a frenzy of transatlantic and US correspondence and making the relevant telephone calls in search of business leads in Atlanta, I commenced an intensive cultivation of the local business community:

- British Consulate General
- Businesses
- Banks
- "Big Eight" accounting firms
- International law firms
- Management consultants
- Georgia Department of Industry & Trade

They were all charming and receptive, lunching me at the best clubs and restaurants and providing an ever-widening network of contacts and ideas. Though I was mainly expecting to contract with UK companies looking West, would there not be similar prospects for US companies wishing to enter markets in Europe? Widely circulated reprints of my article "The Managing

Director's Sleepless Night" in the *London Chamber of Commerce* journal (see Appendix) must surely show that this managing director was sufficiently used to coping with companies' manufacturing and outside problems to qualify him for alter ego projects, but after several months of frenetic effort, still no business came.

Shoestring transatlantic saga

It was time to do more digging in England. Ever more conscious of my depleting finances, for only the cost of the petrol we drove a Chrysler due for delivery by an agency in New York, with hopes for useful meetings in Washington en route. When the Chrysler broke down and forced us to pay for an overnight Greyhound bus to Manhattan, we arrived exhausted and constipated, to be denied the return of our car deposit. The logistics of getting seven pieces of luggage and business documents in safe keeping at Grand Central Station before taking the train to relatives, bearing only overnight necessities would take too long to describe here. Now came the matter of deciding which airline had the cheapest available standby to Heathrow and how to make two days of meetings in Manhattan and New Jersey without spending money. Finally I took a "major decision" – to rent a car for 24 hours in Manhattan, pick up the luggage and drive to a New Jersey meeting before returning the fifty miles to my relatives in Scarsdale. The luggage delivered to JFK at 8.30 a.m. the following morning would allow time to return the car before missing the deadline that would cost another day's rental. Then four more meetings around Manhattan travelling mostly by Shanks's pony, before arriving back at JFK for their overnight standby flight. Until we disembarked from the red-eye, we had no certainty of being met, nor with our house rented out, where we could stay without needing to pay for a hotel. After some waiting, in-laws puffed somewhat breathlessly into the arrivals hall and drove us past our off-limits rented home to their nearby house for a week's hospitality – and where I could telephone for appointments from our host's kitchen. The second week had us "camping" pillar to post between other relatives and meeting client prospects around the country, before we thankfully flew back to the US.

Returning via Baltimore, we collected the Bentley from a ship three months delayed by the Falklands War. The past client's accountant had adamantly refused any compensation for his continued loan of the Toyota. Now we drove south in style, to see the ever-taller pines as we neared Atlanta. In an attempt to save on rent at Tahoe North, every item of household belongings was left with friends around town, in the hope of the management renting to somebody else during our absence. In the event, the management had not bothered to help and we now ran the marathon, bringing all our belongings back from friends' basements, without having benefited from any rent reduction.

By September, still with no assignments, do or die it was now time to go to England again and stay as long as may be necessary to gain some contracts. A security show in New York gave the opportunity to trawl through more worldwide contacts in the industry, resulting in a number of leads to follow up in the UK. Having taken the cheapest hopscotch flight from Atlanta and again staying with relatives outside Manhattan, we stood by for another cheap flight to Heathrow. This was becoming an unpleasant habit. Now more pounding of the motorways and meetings with prospective exporters to the USA.

First contracts

Slowly the spadework of a year's frenetic activity and struggle led to serious discussions. An electronics manufacturer in Twickenham needed representation for its Intrinsic Safety products in the US and negotiated a contract to find manufacturer reps around the country, then negotiate agency agreements and train them. They would help with the expense of a small office to hold their stock in Atlanta and the relevant manager would visit to approve reps as they were coming on line. Back in the security industry, a small manufacturer of microwave detectors on the South Coast provided training in their leading edge perimeter defence Microwave Radar system and agreed a contract for demonstrations to military agencies and larger security system companies nationwide. This would involve lugging heavy equipment on airline trips and in rented cars, setting up and lecturing on the system's capabilities. Many meetings with the British Overseas Trade Board finally led to a market research contract relating to the willingness (or otherwise) of American companies to use the alter ego approach for exports from the US. It had taken a nail-biting year but things were beginning to happen. Finally, after thirteen weeks in England with a ton of documentation, I took three contracts totalling $100,000 back for an early January start!

Princess Anne asks about IMEMCO's business in the USA

Leaping the "No Entry" sign

Confidence rising and renters having departed, we put the house on the market and had most of our furniture shipped to Atlanta for delivery at Tahoe North the day after arriving back. This would enable us to rent unfurnished, halving the rent to $400 a month. Arriving in Atlanta, the Immigration official surveyed our mountain of luggage and asked the usual questions about the purpose and duration of the "visit". At this time, although still on Visitor visas, our income was entirely from the UK and the work would be quite legal. Unsuccessfully, we had already spent $1,000 or so with an attorney on attempts to gain Investor or Treaty Trader visas permitting longer stays than the six months allowable as visitors. Now the man with the rubber stamp held it aloft, insisting, "Y'all have the wrong visa for entering and working in the United States. Take the next plane back to London!"

Careful to avoid any mention of our waiting furniture or the Bentley, over a half hour argument I wore the man down until he relented. "Y'all should have a Treaty Trader Visa – the next time you come, you may have a less sympathetic Immigration Officer." Ready to start $100,000 worth of work, deportation would have really taken the biscuit. Phew! Next priority was some kind of long-term visa.

A low cost office "with services" in a British company's suite permitted a start on the contracts and the spare bedroom reverted to its original purpose. A local secretary transcribed tapes to the extent that she could follow a "British English" accent, and occasional dictation. We really were in business. Already intimately familiar with Atlanta, its suburbs and pastoral environs, taking our time we began to look seriously for somewhere to buy a house. With the pound falling from the recent $2 level to $1.85, the value of our UK house was already down by the equivalent of one bedroom. Nevertheless, Atlanta house prices were much lower and there was considerable choice. The main question was how surely would the business continue and then, how far to risk whatever was left from the sale in England after repaying the bank. Having viewed many properties in various attractive suburbs, we found less expensive new condominiums selling even before they were finished, in a beautiful 30-acre park-like fenced community in elegant Buckhead. Close enough to freeways, shopping malls and all the amenities of town living, complete with lakes, waterfalls, a swimming pool and clubhouse, it was the kind of place people paid dearly to visit for their holidays – as could our children with their families if we could but get in there. By June, the UK house had sold and flaunting my contracts and a 25% deposit, I survived the inquisition by a mortgage lender to buy a unit with two bedrooms and two bathrooms in The Plantation at Lenox. Except for the small matter of gaining permanent resident status, we had become immigrants.

It took another year gazing up at the sword of Damocles hanging over my efforts, and $2,000 more in attorney fees, before we obtained a three-year H-I Visa rejoicing in the description "for Aliens of Distinguished Ability and Merit..." After a decent interval before applying for permanent status we would apply for the coveted green card. The danger of everything folding up under us remained uppermost in our minds and as a last ditch protection, we bought a bijou flat within reach of London – a bolt-hole in case of total failure in America. It also served as a convenient base during UK visits to seek business.

IMEMCO develops

As the first contracts progressed, often to inconclusive end results where the client "chickened out" of the follow up investments that could have brought fulfilment in the US, a pattern began to emerge. Every six months, July/August and December/January, we would visit the UK for a few weeks to pound the motorways, generating a pipeline of prospects that would occasionally mature into a contract. Despite the compelling logic of the alter ego concept, which not a single prospect disputed, getting commitments and cheques remained as slow as pulling teeth without the pinchers. Everybody was willing to offer work on a purely incentive commission basis, but without capital on which to fall back, my only option remained to insist on regular payment of fees against a pre-agreed plan. I really needed a UK based partner to find the business on a commission basis, while contracts were executed in America. I could then also seek business from US companies looking for market entry into Europe on a reciprocally similar basis. With plenty of ex-colleagues and other contacts prized out of the woodwork, several relationships started with a degree of enthusiasm. Many putative projects were investigated and much correspondence was faxed in each direction – mainly without result. None of my partners seemed to have the ability to close business.

Just about every UK visit resulted in one or two contracts, out of an ever longer pipeline of possibilities. Some very limited in the $10,000 range, others in the $60,000 category, while others still would be ongoing retainers that paid the rent. Small advertisements risked in the *Financial Times* proved totally unproductive. It was really down to networking, persistence, persistence and persistence.

The Intrinsic Safety representation project continued for a couple of years, while the Microwave system fizzled after its first phase, when it failed to meet newly updated US specifications and the client would not make the necessary technical changes. An exciting prospect with Computeach to set up computer programmer COBOL training of self-funded students by Distance Learning got under way after a joint market research exercise in Atlanta. Together with a visiting executive, we interviewed and conducted adaptability tests on prospective students in a hotel, leading to a mutual conclusion that a business could follow the success Computeach enjoyed in the Midlands. Now they pressed IMEMCO to open a business using my own funds, with them supplying the materials at reduced rates as for a franchise operation.

Greatly needing the income that would raise my otherwise fee dependent stakes, I brought over some remaining UK funds and hired a manager. During his training visit to the UK he was exhibiting a drinking problem and the previously successful emulation of Computeach's advertising failed to gather any students able to pay for the courses. By the time I fired the manager and licked my wounds, I had lost $17,000. From then I would again only accept fee paid contracts.

BackPak was an ingenious invention by an engineer in Peterborough, the device being attached behind vehicles with a trailer hitch. It could carry 10 cubic feet of cargo or using an alternate platform it carried several bicycles without touching the ground, avoiding the speed restrictions with trailers. Funding of the design was by a company which agreed to a contract for licensing its manufacture in the USA. For $30,000, over several months IMEMCO researched the market among trailer manufacturers and possible competitors, finishing up with a highly interested potential licensee in Atlanta. For a second $30,000, I was contracted to negotiate the license agreement, which also involved testing and focus groups. License agreement details were offered including a minimum payment and royalties, until the megalomaniac company chairman began to ask for ever-higher payments. In the meantime, the focus groups gave equivocal answers and the deal collapsed, leaving me to collect the second fee only after several months of threats to sue. Not a success for British exports, but allowing IMEMCO to continue the business.

An old contact, whose Stevenage company manufactured anti knock sensors took a year to obtain BOTB market research funds, before "leaping" into an investment of a few thousand dollars. This enabled me to present the anti knock sensor in Detroit, for possible specification with new engines under development at GM, Chrysler and Ford. The company's will to embark on serious exporting was not enough to pursue a follow up project.

The Atlanta British Consul Commercial introduced another UK access control systems manufacturer, with a fairly advanced product they had begun to distribute in America. After a training visit to Poole, they agreed a monthly retainer and travel expenses plus commission on sales, adding a contribution to office expenses for an initial six months later extended to a year and beyond. IMEMCO's function was to motivate and increase the distribution outlets and to provide local technical support. They provided good back up support and as I appointed more distributors, sales against deeply entrenched competition slowly began to pick up. The client's ideas then grew beyond IMEMCO's recommendations, when despite being a small company of about 30 people with limited punch and resources, they decided to establish their own US company with full technical and selling capability. They started sending directors and executives over regularly and placed four or five employees in an expensive Atlanta office as if they were IBM. They were clearly on a path to spending half a million Sterling at risk, in the hope of speeding up their sales before it was all spent. Against my advice, rather than keep the original arrangement, they pursued the grand plan until the inevitable happened and they closed it all down. At least IMEMCO was able to buy their fax machine and copier with a variety of other useful office equipment at a knock-down price. Fees and commissions continued for a while and they remained friends, but they had bitten off more than was sensible.

A totally different tack far from my ken resulted in a most interesting contract. An outcrop from Cambridge University Press, the client company published learned journals on cell biology, many of which were sold to universities around America. They needed to find out why American journals' distribution was rising in market share at their expense – and how to take suitable countermeasures. This project again involved proposals first requiring BOTB approval for their financial support of a contract. After some months, a host of their journals arrived in Atlanta and I began to visit university libraries, editorial directors, professors of biotechnology and distribution companies. At Harvard Medical School and at the University of Wisconsin, it soon became apparent that cell biology was developing in the second half of the 1980's toward genetics and the British journals published little in this direction. Furthermore, the prices charged to individual subscribers were equally high to those for libraries, contrary to US practice of heavily discounting individual subscriptions. The latter effect greatly increased the volume of journals ordered, reducing production costs in America – but not in Cambridge. IMEMCO's proposed action plan to generate more scientific papers on genetics and to change the pricing policy was later implemented by the client.

A UK partner with productive clout

A number of UK partners had come and gone over several years, without adding any business to what I generated myself, during my own visits home. With a Georgia Appeal Court Judge's introduction and the help of the Georgia Commissioner for Trade and Industry who leaned on the local Director of Immigration, our Permanent Resident Status was finally granted after five years and a total of $5,000 in legal bills, so the sword of Damocles was at last removed.

A ray of light came with the retirement of an old friend from the Chubb main board. David had no need to earn money, but he was looking to do something interesting and challenging. We agreed to join forces in the mutual manner already envisaged and produced new literature bearing respective photographs, which he distributed, as he also followed up the many slow moving prospects. Before long, his still fresh contacts at Chubb revealed a need to investigate the US market for their new access control system and later for a new digital CCTV recording system that provided pre-alarm pictures. For a couple of years, this contract required identifying prospective users and installers and visiting companies around the security industry in several states of the Union, first alone and returning with a Chubb executive. Chubb awarded successive fixed price contracts, which they repeatedly acclaimed as excellent value for money – although they were based on estimates using the undeclared $1,500 per day fee structure. In the end, in preparation for a public floatation and much to David's chagrin and of the executives who had commissioned IMEMCO's work, new top management at Chubb put an end to most new product development and just about all fee paid outsiders. I had earned well over the period, but new projects were again required.

Projects in the US to UK direction had not prospered at all – even to the extent of an excellent Ohio company getting close to writing a contract. They were due to exhibit in London when news of some IRA bomb activity broke in the US. "Should we cancel?" they asked. Trying not to sound dismissive, I assured them that nobody in England would be changing their business patterns – "After all the Blitz in WWII hardly succeeded in demotivating us". However, they cancelled and any deal was off.

Then, IMEMCO was approached out of the blue, by the newly acquired Tridom division of the great AT&T located close by, within greater Atlanta. Tridom made Small Aperture Satellite Terminals for communications and wanted the best possible help and advice concerning the political as well as technical issues of establishing their systems in the UK. An ex boss from an earlier incarnation later became managing director of Post Office Telephones and oversaw its preparation for privatisation as British Telecom, receiving a knighthood in the process. With a pioneering background in Radar and subsequent industry leadership in that field, he was well known and I had remained in touch, with visits to his house. After retiring, he had continued with consulting work for high profile companies and now I asked whether he would be interested in acting for IMEMCO to help AT&T Tridom. "Only if I can make a worthwhile contribution – and if I can do any travelling First Class", he replied. If he could be satisfied on the first point, the second one would be no great problem and I sent him a formal requirement on which to make a quotation at his none too modest charging rate. Tridom had of course heard of him and were pleased with his continuing access to top politicians and industrialists on which he based his approach to the problems. With a 20% margin added, a contract materialised and paid to IMEMCO in Atlanta, who paid the knight as a subcontractor. What goes around comes around!

Despite all the UK partners' genuine attentions to seeking IMEMCO business, apart from the not insignificant Chubb business gained as a very recent insider, he was unable to gain any other business. Embarrassed, he conceded, "I'm really sorry but I'm not hungry enough to put in the effort that you do". Remaining the greatest of friends with continuing regular contact whenever I was in the UK, he retired from the partnership and IMEMCO (Atlanta) was back to its own devices. However, one further benefit from the Chubb relationship followed, when the Chubb executive came to a US security show and introduced me to another British managing director. His company had the latest developments in video multiplexing and was desperate for a temporary general manager, till their US business in Washington DC became fully functional. This looked very much like my first assignment in Atlanta, but with a larger and faster moving company – based in Manchester.

After introductions and listening to my background, the young managing director almost hugged me with relief. "You are an angel descended from Heaven", he exclaimed and invited me to visit the company for induction into their products, their engineering and their marketing situation. Like the first MD he was running ragged, back and forth between their Manchester and Washington DC offices and urgently needed somebody he could trust to run things without requiring his daily attention. Over a couple of day's introduction in Manchester, a contract was negotiated and I quickly typed the details up on the MD's laptop as he watched. He printed it out and a contract was signed. Back to the US for an early start.

We had agreed that I could continue operating from my Atlanta office, making three-day trips to Washington every week or two accumulating up to nine days per month at $1,000 per day, with all travel and expenses reimbursed. This was my one truly per diem contract, but being the only practical way, it was accepted without argument. Back in the US, I was introduced to the employees on my first visit to Washington. Faintly approaching my past activities as a managing director, dealing with staff handling engineering, system specification, distribution and inside sales, warranty support and all, I was now combining my own travel and telephone marketing activity with overseeing work delegated to the employees. This contract lasted for some nine months, until the client found his permanent manager – who incidentally turned out to be very temporary, once he had made of with some of the contents of the till! However, IMEMCO had made a contribution to getting the company onto a good footing and they moved on – eventually to become a significant force in the US CCTV market.

What else is "impossible"?

The IMEMCO one-man business had now run for approaching ten years, without our starving to death. Beyond establishing a pleasant, if peripatetic life in our adopted city, neither had we saved a fortune. My biggest disappointment was the failure to establish a larger practice with partners operating in the UK and perhaps in the USA.

What lessons can be learned from this venture?

1 With enough versatility and effort, the entrepreneur can build a business against the odds.

2 Lack of finance can be overcome, if he "cuts his coat according to his cloth".

3 International business builds slowly. The Atlantic divides, but can also enable.

4 Client MD's can be their own worst enemy, when they won't listen.

5

CREATE A HANDSOME NEST EGG WITH A ONE-MAN BUSINESS

Create A Handsome Nest Egg With A One-man Business

Case study: Too risky for Angels to invest! "Bootstrap" up the cash mountain – then sell

Conventional wisdom need not always be correct – in the real world. Which MBA course or business textbook would encourage any budding entrepreneur to try the many times proven "impossible"? Surely, there are better and less risky ways of building your pile. "If you have the skills, make sure you have the resources to put into a business." Is that not the best way? Maybe. On the other hand, it also depends on where you have to start.

For historic reasons I had no capital to put into a venture that would require buying expensive stocks, importing them into the USA under my own title and marketing them all over North America. Having found some leading edge, high technology access control equipment for personnel detection made near Heathrow, and some equally advanced and complementary proximity card access systems made in South Africa, I was able to check them out and hopefully negotiate exclusive distribution. Both products were clearly superior to US competition and the landed prices permitted a highly competitive price structure – while retaining substantial margins – well above my business plan's assumptions. I took a deep breath and dived in.

Capital for a start-up?

Without capital, this was clearly not going to be big business any time soon. Even so, in such a large market it was highly desirable to apply some selling clout – enough feet on the ground to apply the necessary sales efforts for the wheel to start turning in short order. My business plan showed that with

$500,000 for marketing and for inventory, in five years I could reasonably expect to be turning over $12m p.a., with contract values ranging between $10,000 and $75,000 or more. With a pessimistic minimum of 27% gross margins assumed, to compete with well calibrated opposition and allowing the necessary selling and other overhead expenses, the plan showed break even in Year Two and net income after taxes of $1.3m in Year Five. Valuing the company at only seven times net earnings, at this five year point, the value of a 15% share holding would be recovered more than five fold – not an unattractive return for an investor?

Never expect venture capitalists to really venture. For them, start-ups are effectively a no-no and while a succession of companies looked seriously at the business plan and did not argue its validity, they all shied away in favour of larger fish, whose evaluation was no less onerous or costly than the $500k investment needed. The big banks, whose small business department minions were delegated to evaluating prospective loans at this level, remained as banks always seemed to be – totally non-entrepreneurial and without commercial acumen. It was beyond them to calibrate that dreadful facet of business – risk. Opportunity does not appear to enter into their thinking and one by one, all the big banks walked away. Then after zipping up to New York, an ex Merryll Lynch high flyer who claimed to know how to raise this kind of money from wealthy "angels" took a few thousand dollars in fees, rewrote the business plan in his own image without changing the numbers and made efforts to find investors – until he went out of business himself and vacated his plush Manhattan offices. I was back to square one.

Jimmy Walker was president of a local community bank with two branches in Atlanta – its name, appropriately, Enterprise National Bank. Since he handled Government guaranteed Small Business Administration (SBA) loans and had known me for a while, we discussed what his bank might be able to offer. "Let me take a look at your business plan, and I'll get back to you." Early the next week, Jimmy called. "I've read your plan John – and you seem to know what you're talking about. I'll be pleased to make you a loan – a line of credit – but don't bother with the SBA, you'll need to give us collateral anyway. We'll look at your collateral – what do you have?" Our partly mortgaged condominium was the only bank-worthy fixed asset I had in the US, and using this collateral, I received a $50,000 line of credit – guaranteed and secured against the considerably higher value condo, my blood and my life. Just one tenth of what I had in mind – affording no possibility of hiring staff or of frequent trips around the US.

Well, I thought, "I have 'some satisfaction'" as Mick Jagger might say, but this was going to be down to a one-man band. Without ever indulging in computer training and amid much cussing and swearing as I learned the hard way, I had begun to get the hang of computer software and my laptop started its long stint of service as the company's work force. Before long into its black 12" x 10" x 2" envelope, I squeezed my sales manager, an office sales coordinator and admin manager, a data base manager, an excellent secretary with automatic telephone dialling and my accountant. Most conveniently, as if permanently connected to my umbilicus, I could take it home every evening for more work after dinner and it went with me on every trip by car or airplane. My little office in Sandy Springs already had fax and phone lines, a photocopier and room for somewhere to sit with a visitor or two, to write and file documents and to demonstrate system hardware. The lease was not too expensive and included air conditioning and lighting. OK, so long as I could pay the mortgage on the condo and the two of us were content to live on a monthly "salary" of $2,000 less tax! Hardly the American Dream, but perhaps with patience – later?

Suppliers, sales and support

Thus putting everything on the line, it was essential to secure exclusivity in North America – exactly what most manufacturers abhor in their desire for an easy way out in the event of disappointing orders. The UK supplier had not seriously considered exports, let alone to the USA and being essentially a small engineering oriented company, did not even have a sales team or manager. Yet their product had no competition in the UK and the US looked like a win-win opportunity. Though the MD was pathologically opposed to exclusive arrangements, I held out the prospects for big bucks and with much reluctance he agreed two years of exclusivity. The South African supplier gave a similarly reluctant brief and I was ready to order my first minuscule stock. Neither supplier had suitably Americanised technical or sales literature and the first long haul was to produce enough ideas and proposals for them to create some usable material. Technical manuals and troubleshooting information had been virtually absent and they now gradually became adequate for the job.

Having experienced some facts of life, I knew that with high tech products, technical support is an essential capability and in the absence of funds to hire a support engineer with a travel budget, the suppliers and I had to be content with a deal I had negotiated with a friend who was a security systems integrator. This was for his engineers to be trained and to provide the support as required, in return for 2% commission on sales. At the same time, besides having to learn the products in-depth for selling purposes, I was prepared to use my engineering knowledge and experience to field most support requests – by telephone.

A second UK industry supplier, of tamper proof security bags, looked like providing another, perhaps larger slice of business and on the strength of that, I was able to recruit an old attorney friend onto my Board along with another business man from North Carolina – neither of whom were willing to put any useful cash into the business in return for their respective 30% of the $100 share capital. However, the security bags' supplier who had indicated his willingness to finance a sales executive decided that he wanted the US distributor to provide the additional funds and, since neither of the "partners" was willing to put cash in, this supplier reneged. I bought back each partner's thirty $1 shares as they took to their heels. I was back to the one-man band.

Without adequate funds for the regular trips around the US normally associated with national marketing, I had to content myself with sporadic trips when the prospects looked sufficiently compelling and in the main, relied on mail shots and the telephone. Existing contacts in the industry provided the beginnings of a database, but at around $4,000 per page, advertising was out! Using only two or three of the dozen security publications where competitors advertised most months, the line of credit could be used up in no time. However editorial coverage was free and I set about creating press releases with photographs and wrote articles for publication, which all began to appear in the right magazines with satisfying regularity. More satisfying was the flow of "bingo card" enquiries these generated. The database grew and grew, to the point where I was just about keeping up with the responses – and rapidly using up my stock of literature. Follow up problems were sumpt'n else. It takes no effort to circle a Reader Service Card, but when I called to get reactions to the fuller technical literature, if I managed to reach the person concerned by the third or fourth attempt, often as not they had forgotten they had enquired! Then they would claim the literature never arrived and "Would you mind sending another set?" With stocks and my time depleting and the high cost of mailing heavy packages, I had to swallow hard to avoid giving a dusty answer.

Manufacturers' representatives working on commission seemed to be the only affordable way to increase the number of feet on the ground and I recruited a few around the US and Canada – who also wanted exclusivity in their States. More training and more literature to provide, but even at the unusually high 10% commission I offered, many were unwilling to sustain the necessary effort required to pioneer a new product, when their time could be more productively spent with their existing and well established portfolios. Promises and their training notwithstanding, even regular tweaking and chasing still left them asking elementary questions and required my personal time to compensate for insufficient effectiveness with customers. Bingo cards sent to them for personal follow up in their localities went into a vacuum – to the point where I was calling into their areas myself. In the quest for this month's commissions, they did not have the patience to make the several calls required to reach a prospect before it cooled.

Committed, I was now spending real money mounting my first exhibition booths at security shows in New York and San Antonio TX, with help from visiting supplier executives. Our tiny 10 ft. booth remained busy and the response to the equipment and its demonstration was encouraging enough to bolster our hopes – though we did not receive nor expect to receive any immediate orders. The suppliers went back home in high sprits and waited for the orders to pour in.

Much to the suppliers' chagrin, most of the technical support remained with me, my telephone and fax – and on occasion, my soldering iron. Orders were slowly beginning to appear, but after more exhibitions, at least two in each year, these were still nowhere near enough to satisfy either the suppliers, or the financial needs of the business. "All I want is more business for less effort" was the UK supplier's fanciful approach to winning export markets. "I don't want you to sell anything but products as we make them – don't keep asking for changes [to suit American customer's needs]." I was the distributor and it was up to me to sell, import, support and to pay all the bills.

Survival

At the start of year three, both suppliers refused to extend exclusivity – leaving me with the danger that they may appoint competing distributors, which could confuse and dilute the business, even in the large US market. By the nature of distribution, the exhibition locations, which varied from state to state and the national nature of the security media, enquiries came from all over the territory. Any dilution of exclusivity could quickly kill the enterprise and I was now working without contractual exclusivity but happily, the ill afforded effort required by non US-based suppliers to find more distributors was a saving grace. More importantly, the UK supplier had hired a capable sales manager with a marketing budget, and the support level for the US effort quickly leapt from the abysmal to the excellent. Sales literature and manuals were produced in accordance with requirements in the US and speedy responses to technical queries and delivery needs became the norm. Requests for product changes to suit the American market were no longer automatically regarded as a mere nuisance and they began to result in important modifications. Thereafter, distributor and supplier developed an easy and trusting relationship, which put the threat of competing distributors onto the back burner.

With care, I had insistently negotiated 60 day payment terms, so while I was able to bring customer receipts in ahead of my own nominal 30 day payment terms, the cash flow problem was essentially a matter of paying for overheads. The nature of capital projects involved six or more weeks delivery of fairly large orders, so pre-delivery payments actually enabled me to obtain substantial funds well in advance of delivery, with a highly beneficial effect on cash flow once the order rate began to rise.

To sceptical American buyers, the Laws of Physics change when crossing the Atlantic, and one by one, they had to be convinced that the product really performs as claimed. Besides this, they were scared to the point of paranoia by fears of being left high and dry in the event of a fault in the field. On this account, I could assure them of 24 hour spares deliveries from my stock, or at worst 48 hour delivery direct from the UK. Flying all over the country to sort out every query – mostly self-induced by careless installers – would be prohibitive for my support contractor or myself and I quickly developed a technique of telephone support and "hand holding" which permitted rapid solutions to any problems in the field and successful completion of their installations. This is of course where the reliability and the consistency of the product is of cardinal importance – and give credit to the suppliers, this was so. As the first two or three years progressed, it became possible to boast to all who made heavy weather of their distrust for imported products, that every installation had been completed smoothly, without requiring a site visit and, equally important, there had not been a single failure in the field.

Slowly, a reputation for integrity was created, but now came another real-world problem. Enquiries would come from a system integrator, who would bid against other installers to the end user. So long as they met a minimum specification, not only did the product's superior performance come second to price, another consideration was that the competitors were much better known and established, with reference installations in areas where I had never yet sold. One Pittsburgh integrator pursued me as much as I pursued them for over a year, while trying to sell to an end user. After a longer than usual period of silence, I called to see how the project was progressing. "I'm sorry Juuuuhn, but we purchased a system from your competitor. You didn't have an installation in Pittsburgh to show my customer – but your competitor had two right in town." A two hour drive to his nearest installation in New Jersey was too much – it's always the least effort solution that wins.

After a card access installation by the tech support company for Bell South in Atlanta, their first high profile order for the UK product came from Whirlpool, some two years after they saw it in San Antonio. At their Tulsa OK manufacturing plant, its installation (by the main competitor's parent company) went smoothly and a fortnight later, Whirlpool's security director called to arrange for a second installation at his corporate headquarters. New York's soon to be Mayor, billionaire Mike Bloomberg, was looking for a similar system in his Park Avenue headquarters and after one of those 6.30 a.m. flights from Atlanta, I was demonstrating the personnel detection equipment to the dynamo chairman of Bloomberg LP. It took another year before the first system order was received from Bloomberg's New Jersey installer and as this was followed by several repeat orders, the ability to give powerful references became a reality. Now I could boast both reliably high performance and repeat customers, to the still unbelieving new prospects I was continually chasing.

However by this time, the $50,000 line of credit was not only fully used, so was my MasterCard's greatly increased credit limit and I was renting out our small UK flat, bringing the proceeds to Atlanta each month, along with our UK pension, to keep afloat. With these subsidies and by selling half of our few shares, then the Bentley, as well as reducing my $2,000 salary take from the company, we held body and soul together, as the sales curve struggled uphill. Nevertheless, by years three and four, the effect of my intense flag waving around the market began to bring additional high profile accounts:

- The US Olympics
- Bloomberg
- Whirlpool
- Bristol Myers Squibb
- The US Navy
- Blue Cross/Blue Shield
- Various newspapers
- Hershey Chocolate
- Harley Davidson
- Repeat orders from QVC and others

Now the high margins and early cash flows began to eat away at the debt and suddenly, the line of credit loan was being whittled down to a shadow of its previously fulsome level. I was showing quite handsome profits and a relatively healthy balance sheet.

More blindness in banks

Jimmy Walker sold his bank to a larger bank out of Birmingham AL and I duly went to see the local branch manager. "Regents Bank can't renew your line of credit – it's against our policy to lend to companies that don't have a five year history of rising profits." Flabbergasted, I oozed reason, "Excuse me, but since the last two of our five years from starting up, we have been making increasing profits – the line of credit is nearly all repaid. Another three or four months and we won't need it at all", I protested. No amount of demonstrating the turnaround, performance and prospects had any effect on the bureaucrat and he gave me 90 days to find another bank. There was no option but to look for another small community bank that might have an inkling about business. After some searching and with Jimmy Walker's help, I located the First Security National Bank, also with just a couple of branches and the chairman agreed to take us on, keeping the line of credit going. After all of the usual statutory formalities and documents, guarantees, notes giving them liens all the assets, with the credit card already paid off, he took up the $15,000 that remained necessary to stay in business.

On the way up and managing progress

Now, positively on the up and up, the loan was quickly repaid and I began to build an increasingly healthy money market balance earning a modestly useful interest. From year six, I rarely held less than $100,000 in this account – a sum Regents Bank could have been holding and using for loans to make them profit. The more fools they proved to be and good riddance. For the first time, I was able to increase the company's marketing spend, pay for larger and better equipped booths in security shows, print my own improved sales literature and no longer look at how to cut each telephone bill. I could travel with an easier conscience and no longer begrudge the hotel costs involved. As soon as the spare cash allowed, I bought a new looking Ford Crown Victoria with almost Bentley level comforts – and much lower running costs.

Keeping all these balls in the air with little help from manufacturers' reps stretched me as tight as a violin string and to continue mixing metaphors, had me coiled like an over wound clock spring. The database now extended to over four thousand names, of which a couple of hundred were active at any time, involving hours of telephone time each day. To keep up with the rapidly escalating volume of information and the continuing situation changes as discussions progressed, memory would clearly never ensure that a prospect could be properly progressed, that mistakes be avoided and that a record be maintained of each prospect's contact history. Apart from that, if anybody else were to join the business, now a distinct possibility, they would need to have reliable reference material at the touch of a computer key. My database software already kept all prospect and customer contact details in easily managed lists and groups that enabled selective mail shots to be readily assembled. Particularly before security exhibitions, these mail shots were targeted at the most likely prospects, architects, engineers, end users, system integrators and existing customers, weighted by their proximity to the shows' locations. By judiciously modifying the layout and features of the software, I was able to produce a relational database of information about specific calls, visits and discussions, which were unique to each prospect.

It was now possible to call up lists of people requiring a call today or this week and to check on missed follow-ups and so to call prospects in order of priority. Automatic dialling of the embedded telephone numbers speeded the making of calls and permitted details of the conversation to be typed into the record simultaneously with the conversation, keeping hands free by using a speakerphone. The next follow up date then entered ensured that the prospect came up after a well-chosen interval and there was no real excuse for mishandling any call. Anybody else coming into the business could take any prospect over, with a full history on the screen in front of him.

Keeping track of projects being pursued required more detail:

- Customer
- Project name
- Equipment content
- System integrators bidding the project
- Expected date
- Probability of gaining the order

- Cost of purchasing and landing
- Value to quote
- Gross margin to be earned

These were entered into another database as a tabulation, with totals for all the numerical information summed at the bottom. This also factored the order values and the project costs by the estimated probability of gaining the order and on a single screen or printed page, I now had the likely business outcome between selected dates in terms of (factored) sales, equipment import costs and gross margins. This pipeline became the forward plan and a bible alongside the accrual based accounting system for running the business. Even for a one-man band, it was essential to have such a professional set of management information. The two databases could be brought onto a split screen, permitting immediate cross-reference between projects and the state of discussion with the relevant contacts. Plus, on my laptop I could check details at home and while airborne en route for a customer visit, or a show, and for continued pursuit while in England.

As profits reached the $150,000 to $200,000 p.a. range and the pipeline showed future growth that could easily double the business in a couple of years, the question of creating a nest egg could be faced.

Grow fast now or save for retirement?

I had a choice between hiring help to grow the business even faster or, if I could continue to handle the workload, to take dividends and save towards a nest egg. Adding staff would bring profits down before they could create the desired increase beyond current levels and there was always the risk that a new person turns out to be unsuitable, or does not stay. Keeping the highly profitable one-man band and saving cash seemed the surest way to build a nest egg, and with the forward plan looking so good, it could be within the bounds of possibility that I could even sell the business.

Due to already intense US competition and excessive delay in updating their system, the South African supplier's card access system had petered out some time earlier and only the UK personnel detection equipment egg remained in my basket. That had always been an uncomfortable reality, though even in the absence of formal exclusivity, the supplier's support had been faithfully sustained as he saw the steady build-up of his US export business. The US market was now producing over half of their exports and about 20% of their turnover, so he was keen to see continuation in the event I retired. Always playing tough, they made many dark comments about their ability to restart with somebody else or by opening up in the US themselves, but deep down they knew that their risk of losing the US market altogether – and a packet of money – was substantial. After all, in marginal terms the US sales were generating all of their profit. They therefore began to accept the idea of my assuring continuity by selling the company to a suitably capable person or a larger company.

Selling the business

Without result, I had already made a few approaches, which had to be discreet and outside my customer spectrum, to avoid the business being killed stone dead by a loss in confidence if news got out. It would be cardinal for the supplier to have full confidence in any new potential owner before he would offer the distribution rights – and he was still pathologically opposed to exclusivity. Without exclusivity, no prospect would for a moment risk his money, nor make the change from his current job or business. Between a rock and a hard place, I began to negotiate the terms of a potential exclusive agreement, which allowed the supplier to terminate in the event of sales targets being missed. Potential owners unanimously wanted a minimum of five years, but it was possible that a two-year period with rights to terminate exclusivity within a five-year agreement might be acceptable. After two years, the relationship may well have settled down sufficiently for the contract to remain locked in a bottom drawer, as mine had been for the previous several years. In my other twenty-four hours I also started a serious search for buyers.

A good friend introduced a pair of reserve US Marines helicopter pilots and a security guarding company executive seeking their own business, who looked both energetic and capable. The relationship built well – to the point that when I was hospitalised for surgery, they attended the office, made customer follow up calls and brought me up to date while in hospital and rehab. This was beginning to look really promising and they undertook to make a proposal, but their offer was entirely based on payment out of earnings from the business and with no up front payments to ensure their continued performance, I finally had to decline. Six months had been wasted.

Among my many Atlanta business friends was a highly professional executive who specialised in company acquisitions and disposals. His business was mostly with much larger companies; he had just completed a $50m deal, but for his own reasons he liked to dabble in smaller companies (perhaps they are where real people are found) and the hopes for something nearer one hundredth of the size attracted him. I paid an initial $500 search fee, contracting to pay a success fee of up to $30,000 if the proceeds from a sale reached over $350,000. With the pipeline database indicating potential for sales doubling to over $1m in short order and the cash flows brought by gross margins of around 45%, we both thought the company would fetch quite a lot more. With the aid of his web-based capabilities, using a suitable outline description of the business and its financial prospects over five years, a succession of potentially interested parties were winkled out of the woodwork. These then received enough details to whet the appetite and those who signed confidentiality agreements were then sent full product, market and business information.

The constantly increasing list of prospects gradually narrowed down to a few with genuine intentions, who came to the small office for initial product viewings and information. The first serious negotiation with a Florida company's president reached the point of an acceptable Letter of Intent promising a substantial up front payment and this led to a joint visit to the supplier in England. This was apparently to the prospect's satisfaction and the supplier promised to dispatch a completed five-year exclusive distribution agreement for his signature on our return to the USA. The final Asset Purchase Agreement was completed and signed, requiring only the signed distribution agreement document for a closing. This languished over a period of several weeks as the supplier's pen failed to provide enough ink for his signature. Suddenly before the agreed closing date, the buyer changed his mind and the deal was off. Another six months had been wasted, and mutual recriminations with the supplier only made things worse.

The business continued its upward path, now a few months from the start of year ten. Was this the time to give up, retire and let the business be frittered away? I paid another $500 to restart my search. My tenth American Society of Industrial Security trade show, back in San Antonio TX, was coming up in October – with my first double sized booth and much improved displays, plus the supplier's MD and a sales person to help. The usual search process had brought forth three more prospects, some of which came to see the products and the personalities at the show. Still more prospects were coming to sample the trough and soon after returning to Atlanta, I had three highly motivated prospects vying to buy my company. After numerous meetings and many emails and phone calls, there were three competing Letters of Intent to consider, and I knew which one I preferred; not that I could make the choice, unless the supplier agreed.

The supplier set his heart on one he had met in San Antonio, a smart operator but not my first choice. This was both on the grounds of limited technical knowledge and due to a greater part of his offer being dependent on his own ability to grow the business, as compared with another with top-level technical knowledge, who offered fewer conditions in meeting a similar total price. The other two prospects were literally pleading for equal consideration and offered to fly to England at their own risk and expense, to meet the supplier. He went as far as holding long telephone conversations with each and agreed that they were all suitable but would not agree to take the time for these meetings. It had to be the man from Texas – who really wanted ten years exclusivity!

Nevertheless, they compromised on five years, with some caveats concerning sales performance which could allow exclusivity to be rescinded, and after much negotiation and my attorney accumulating substantial charges, we signed and closed the deal to purchase the goodwill and the tiny inventory. A very substantial six-figure sum went into my bank account and after paying the finder's full fee and allowing for a large cut by the US tax authorities, I shipped the balance home for the nest egg. During a training and handover period, it was positively satisfying to see the new owner occupy my desk and chair of long vintage and to spend time in his new Texas office filled with the Atlanta furniture and equipment. After four months of transition, my eighty-hour weeks finally ceased. At the age of 73 I had made a clean exit and the business could continue.

What lessons can be learned from this case study?

1 Nothing, but nothing is impossible – even from a standing start.

2 Don't rely on acumen or help at large or even medium-sized banks.

3 Competitive, reliable products with healthy margins can be found, to compete in the US.

4 A one-man band can present a full company image, with the aid of a laptop computer, if sufficiently targeted and intelligent energy is applied.

5 North America including Canada and Mexico and even South America can be serviced.

6 Competing in the USA requires the service to appear all-American.

7 Favourable terms of trade can be obtained, leading to a healthy bank balance.

8 Professional accrual accounting and cash flow control are essential.

9 Plan ahead on the basis of constantly analysing the business numbers.

10 Be prepared to give what it takes to drive a business to succeed.

11 The goodwill of a business can be sold for significant cash.

6

PRINCIPLES FOR TURNAROUND MANAGEMENT

Principles For Turnaround Management

There is no simple formula for turning red ink into black, and the way of going about it will certainly be different for the many types of business. Turnarounds, particularly in smaller companies, are essentially an entrepreneurial activity and the principles are probably no more than common sense management. Nevertheless, the way in which success or failure depends on the central role of the managing director and on his personal involvement will be somewhat different in a large company. However, experience even in very large companies has shown that the stamp of the managing director is often visible throughout the organization and in its commercial attitudes.

Some reasons for impending doom

For a true entrepreneur, maybe the deeper the crimson the more exhilarating the challenge, if dicing with doom is his favourite pastime. Imagine the scenario in a smallish manufacturing company of, say, 75 employees. A balance sheet deficit held up by high interest loans, a loss and stock write-off almost equal to a much reduced year's turnover, tax owing on better years, plus outstanding debts for legal and other services and continuing trading losses thumping away with every stroke of ill-managed machinery in a factory. Cash and survival are always on the knife-edge of the overdraft limit. I have demonstrated that such a company can be saved.

To be mainly dependent on one market is a good a way as any to get into troubled waters. Among other fundamental reasons for such a 'red' situation can be excessive product orientation – where too many clever products are made because they are interesting, without clear defining the nature or extent of differing markets. This criticism may seem good textbook stuff, but coupled with unnoticed shifts in the market and insufficient forward planning, this describes all too well, a common situation among the most technically innovative of enterprises.

Simple, practical reasons include a factory making everything twice over, while design engineers mastermind the manufacturing processes in a subordinate works and wrong bookings in the factory, resulting in poor costing information. That in turn can produce little factual basis for forward cost estimates. Inadequate stores records may at first seem to save effort and money in a small company, but the resulting absence of proper stock control is even more costly. More investment in tooling and capital equipment could potentially save many times the cost of inefficient production. Then there are products going to markets which are too disparate for economic selling activity. The principal practical constraint in such cases will always be funds; the cash flow will always be on a knife-edge. Perhaps another must in these circumstances is a steady nerve.

The likelihood of turning a company round could depend on some skilled people already being there, together with some good products and promising ideas. A few of these may be producing the existing level of business, but new products may well be needed to stimulate the growth required for profitability. Assuming that the existing products in their limited sphere and specialisation are doing a good job, cash flow and its maintenance by timely cash collection from customers/debtors is a top priority. They would gain no advantage from turning the boat over, by being too uncooperative in paying their bills.

Since speed and decisiveness are of the essence, the managing director will demand full freedom of action and a well-defined financial carrot – which may well then hang just over the advancing precipice, to ensure the required tender loving care.

First principles

Private venture R&D is the stuff from which great things emerge, so long as it is written off as it is spent, and monthly accounts must record 'actuals', not 'provisions' on a plausible accounting basis. Poor accounting can create a surreptitious disguise for coming bombshells.

The turnaround entrepreneur's axiomatic next given is absolute resolution, that under no circumstances could he countenance the possibility of failure. Obstacles and difficulties are there for only one purpose; to be overcome. As already stated in other chapters, any wall presents only a limited obstruction and by measuring its height and by analysing the optimum way to climb or circumvent it, the obstruction will soon be left behind. He has to have a personal involvement in the detailed character of the business, including in-depth understanding of the products, their application and the skills involved in their manufacture and design. He will keep his finger on every pulse and never tolerate a customer being let down.

Thus, he will decree a clear and consistent policy, which must be equally clear to those inside and outside the company. At the same time there has to be flexibility and willingness to change the policy as situations change. Speed of reaction and full and constant two-way communication are of the essence. The MD has to exhibit absolute integrity as well as fairness in all dealings with employees and in the market. Again, good communications and easy accessibility – no ivory towers. What is more, he should lead from the front, especially in marketing.

Building for tomorrow is a must

This has to be so, even while struggling to survive and it is naturally the most difficult thing to do while funds are short. It involves spending badly needed cash on product and business development, on marketing and on detailed professional accounting, even when the company may be down to a few dozen employees. The financial position always has to be in the MD's briefcase or on his laptop computer, including details like the invoicing due this week, orders due and cash due in and out, however far that briefcase or laptop and its owner are from home.

Every penny of turnover is needed to stay afloat and to recover overheads in the short term, so it is difficult to cut any product until other sources of turnover can take its place. Following the determination and the definition of markets, which take time to educate and seduce, more time is needed to assess and to rationalise products. It is also necessary to assess and to decide about existing managers, whether to replace any or to make the best of them. The effect on morale of keeping them or of removing any could be positive or negative because of action or inaction. Another constraint will be that there are only 28 hours in each of the week's 10 working days!

Basic policy decisions always depend on the nature of a business and its particular situation. However, some clear points arise.

- **Products**
  There will be some which are clearly mainline. As far as priorities are concerned, others, which are of smaller consequence but still contribute towards that vital turnover and profitability, will be allowed to sink or swim.

- **Type of overhead structure**
  To cope with tomorrow as well as the present, this should be designed to allow for the shape intended for the company in the medium term. This could be argued to entail an excessive overhead, but the decision depends on the complexity of the product/market spectrum in the plan, rather than on the size of the company. In the light of this criterion and considering the prices recoverable from the market at attainable volumes, a conscious decision should preferably err on the side of a higher overhead.

- **Investment**

  How much private venture R&D does the company need and could it afford to keep a sound engineering team together? When sales volume is all-important, how best to invest in this and should they go for ambitious export promotion? Should they broaden, or deepen the product base from components to systems, which may have a stronger lever on the market, but need, say, a new electronic engineering capability?

- **Management team**

  What level of managers could they afford or can they possibly afford to have anything but the best? In a small company, managers need to be capable of working down at the grass roots on jobs they would normally delegate; at the same time, if the future is to become one of significant growth, managers should be able to see the wood for the trees, in a professionally analytical way. What of the style of management? Should it be personalised by the MD, with delegated freedom of action and regular progressing of subordinates or be management by committee – ever so slowly producing little 'camels' of decisions?

- **Should the loss making company be cut back?**

  If it is essential, what should be cut? No real functions can go, yet in a small company the only way to reduce some departments by 30% is to cut off an arm or a leg. The owner of the limb is probably already carrying out several such functions. Multi-skilled managers, staff and supervisors are perhaps the best way of keeping numbers down to a few highly interested and motivated people. It is certainly essential to run a tight ship, where everybody is perhaps just a little too tightly stretched and some will fall by the wayside. With a tight ship, the duplication of more than one person attending a meeting or travelling on a visit has to be avoided, so that everybody is working in his own area of responsibility most of the time. Trips have to be "three birds with one stone" affairs; for the same fare can often cover two or three more stops, countries, etc.

The MD must coordinate marketing

The luxuries, like Christmas cards, are easy to give up when it's that or the wages. Savings on how facilities like heat, light, postage, telephones and travelling are used have some beneficial effect and importantly, they affect the psychology of the employees' attitudes, when things are tight. Management would normally prefer to concentrate more and do fewer things better, by cutting out the sink-or-swim products, but this is difficult while the marginal effect of this turnover makes the difference between profit and loss. And since selling and making these products requires little management attention, perhaps they should stay. Sometimes they grow into mainline products – or perhaps they always were, but were misjudged.

For dynamism in a small tightly knit, tightly stretched company, a marketing policy which is closely coordinated by the MD may be the most effective. If the latter's professional strengths lie in other disciplines, a top-thinking marketing man will need to do this in the closest cooperation with the MD. Of course, while the company activity level allows it to be feasible, this one man (spending 50% of his 28-hour day) can be highly effective, particularly if he happens to be a natural salesman at the same time.

In this role, the entrepreneurial MD must have his continually improving assessment of the market's requirements and the corresponding product definitions and cost/price targets at his fingertips (and he must communicate about this with the sales and engineering departments). He must steer design specifications in the direction of features, which are important to users, and monitor the progress of new designs to ensure that they reflect the requirement as it (or understanding of it) changes. Commercial policy, above all pricing, has to be judged in the light of intimate knowledge of all these factors, including the competition, types of sales outlet and buying structures. Important secondary influences on buying decisions in the market include the potential and performance of overseas agents and distributors, national and international standards and even politics.

Leadership should be from the front

For rapid application of a coherent, practical, yet flexible policy, the shortest cut seems to be for one man to cope somehow with both the detail and the broad brush. His personal leadership of capable sales engineers and their pursuit of sales leads, their presentation of the company's image, advertising themes and technical sales literature, even the choice and presentation of engineering test reports for market consumption, these can all be coordinated by also doing part of the work, as well as directing it – leading from the front.

With the aid of his financial controller, the MD must be close to the costing and overhead relationships in the budget and in the profit and loss account. With these go the margins or contributions provided by each product, without which knowledge, the marketing policy decisions may be ill-founded. Break even levels of invoicing and cash flow must be well to the fore, along with the debtors/creditors generated this month, last month, etc. The mysteries of monthly stock movements will remain so (until the truth of stock-taking catches up) unless the accounts department is persuaded to break the figure down into its constituent parts – for each major product area.

Perhaps most important is the regular 'honest look' analysis of how direct labour is utilised. Was this or that overspend caused by a slow operator, or was it really the fault of a wrong production method, or poor design, or rectification or was the estimate bad in the first place? Should labour time have been booked to rectification, or to indirect work unrelated to the job in question, or to waiting time? These smoke screens are excellent at hiding the realistically achievable cost – and they cover up a lot of waste.

Capital expenditure decisions in this environment require analysis against simple criteria of cost saving or practical necessity. Subject only to short- to medium-term cash flow constraints (or ability to find financing), spending can be rapidly agreed and implemented. Not having to obtain approval from a cautious, distant board of directors is an independent enterprise's saving grace. Positive decisions for capital expenditure can also be good for morale.

The position and progress of sales and orders on perhaps a weekly as well as the usual monthly basis helps to keep the MD's adrenalin flowing and to apply appropriate pressures to correct or take advantage of a dynamic situation. Their relationship to budget and to updated forecasts of profit and cash flow closes the information loop and may highlight required action to increase pressure on sales, engineering or production; on the other hand they will sometimes provide the evidence which permits the go-ahead on a capital or R&D project.

Product and market decisions and risk

If you are going to argue that your expensive product is really cheaper to use and install than the competitor's low-priced one, your arguments need to be clarified and coordinated for consistent use by all concerned. Along with these points go, for example, the options of product variants, system configurations, price variations with quantities and delivery, all of which can be continually analysed and prepared for the armoury of negotiating arguments. All these also go back to the many details from all the various departmental disciplines, with which the MD or top marketing man must be intimately familiar.

Since only most of the detail can be there (preferably 95%) – in mind or on paper – whether negotiating in Coventry or California, the full use of instant communications, as far as they are available, can be cheap at the price. Time zone differences can actually be an advantage, as in New York, if the normal working day is fully occupied with meetings, one can call England between the shower and breakfast and call the customer in California before a slightly delayed evening meal. So long as the candle is flexible in the middle, it can be burned at both ends for reasonably useful periods. In a survival and emergence-from-doom situation, events happen fast, and it is easy to give some things too little consideration, particularly when trying to do a number of things at the same time. A potentially critical pitfall while fighting for new customers with all the effort and concentration which that entails, is to take for granted the continued satisfaction of a long-standing customer. This is one area where the teamwork and watchfulness of all concerned with the market are vital.

Estimates of time to achieve objectives, particularly matters like bringing a product to the market or the period required to obtain market acceptance, or obtaining the original equipment contract, or the rate of production build-up, tend to be optimistic. Similarly when budgeting, it is important to distinguish clearly between a plausible sales target, the sales level one is confident in achieving, and a budget against which to plan expenditures. It is also embarrassing, if not worse, to promise the bank to reduce the overdraft in a given time – and then not to achieve it. At the same time, there is the pitfall of being so cautious and pessimistic in forecasting that if you do not cut your own throat, the financial institutions will. You will commit non-financial hara-kiri, if you accept anything but the complete and the best job from managers and staff.

Risks need to be well calculated. To have any chance of turning red into black, an MD has to be optimistic, particularly as seen by others, but preferably also by temperament. He must also be a realist in his inner thoughts and decisions. This means the taking of risks fairly often, but always consciously – and the risks must be well calculated. It certainly pays to budget in detail, even on the basis of sales forecasts which must be largely speculative. Budgeting of labour and material purchasing requirements needs to be in sufficient detail, to make them consistent with the sales forecasts and also for all overhead areas. This will allow analysis and reasoning for better budgeting next year, even if in the event, the sales volume and the mix are different from the forecast. It also provides a yardstick for financial and cost control with the monthly accounts.

Looking beyond the limitations of the home market with a set of new product lines gives an extra order of magnitude in market potential. For a company which is struggling to achieve enough sales volume to crush the overhead rate and provide needed marginal cost benefit and profit, this can be the saving grace. Also, the diversity of markets reduces vulnerability to national economies, strikes and similar forces majeures.

The biggest problem, apart from spreading limited resources too thinly, is the allied one of obtaining good enough market research data. In the absence of unaffordable professional market research investigations, this is again where the MD's deep personal involvement and front-line presence can provide many of the answers to questions, which in any case sometimes only become apparent to the man on the spot.

In most businesses involving technology, product development must be continuous if the desired future is to have any prospect of materializing. Products must be moulded to suit changing market requirements and new products are necessary to supplement the capability of a range or a system; also to anticipate obsolescence and competition. In a small company transmuting from survival to expansion, speed is still of the essence. It may therefore sometimes be better to get the product to the market with reasonable despatch than to have a perfectly planned launching, if that would be too late. The ragged edges of a hurried introduction can be painful and costly later, but clear commercial thinking can indicate where the priorities should be in particular cases. An opportunity lost can leave a permanent gap.

When tomorrow arrives

If success is assumed to be the only possibility, we can only plan for a tomorrow, which will require a full supporting cast of the company functions to be involved in running the show on a bigger scale. For this reason, and to cope with the hazards of today, not only should managers be chosen for their self-motivation and technical qualities, but they should also have experience of larger company operations. It follows that professional systems need to be installed from the start (perhaps in simplified form) to provide regular and full information for accounting, costing, purchasing and stock control, for production control, the processing of enquiries, orders and invoices, without forgetting design, drawing office and modification procedures and the maintenance and safekeeping of records; likewise, for testing, inspection, quality control, concessions, feedback, etc.

If this means a smaller number of direct operatives than overhead staff in the company, it may seem a strange way of turning red into black – but so be it. So long as the markets will bear the resulting costs at the survival turnover level, once sales pass that critical threshold, the recovery from extra sales greatly surpasses any further need for increases in overheads. With management systems operating in simple but expandable form and with a tightly stretched staff, good communications can help to produce effectiveness with reasonable efficiency. When (not if) the expansion comes, the system will be reasonably able to handle the greater rate of information flow and the greater need for professional control.

Organisation for the future will also provide visible evidence on which managers and staff can base their aspirations for career development, without which the rigours and risks of being with the company today may not be worth tolerating. For the sake of their future and the company's future, profit and cash flow today must be constantly balanced against the demands for investment, which will underpin the prospects for tomorrow. In the end, it will be on people that the fortunes of the company will entirely depend, and managers should be encouraged to improve their training level and those of their staff. Their own rewards should also be geared to the success of the enterprise through profit-based bonuses which could ideally reach right through the organization in proportion to responsibility. 'Ideally' in this context means that there needs to be enough profit and cash flow to allow the payment of bonuses which are big enough after tax to be a worthwhile reward for extra efforts.

Many of the principles enumerated here may not be optimum, once the situation is firmly in the black and when continuing or accelerating growth has become the main objective. Some degree of risk-taking and short cuts may not only become unnecessary, but in more complex operations, might result in costly mistakes. Similarly, the personalised management approach will probably result in company indigestion, so managers must then be allowed the maximum scope for participation in major decisions and authority for their own departmental decision-making.

Major decisions will more often become those of a management team, where the MD's judgment is based on specialist advice from department heads, who will have looked deeper into the separate issues than he could now do himself. These decisions will, however, still be his to make and at his risk if they are wrongly taken. If he is to use his experience and knowledge of the business to do more than count votes at meetings, he must still stay well away from ivory towers. In addition, there is now the ability, and a great need, to concentrate on the longer term planning of the business and the moulding of the present into the future.

To apply these principles for effecting a company turnaround, the MD must intrinsically be an entrepreneur, with experience and wisdom to make the necessary rapid judgements and take the corresponding actions. In the context of a relatively small, yet complex company, he must be a man of many skills and his determination to succeed will only be matched by his stamina.

How may we summarise the principles for survival and turnaround?

1 With sufficient determination, skill and versatility, the impossible turnaround can be made to happen. There must never be any acceptance of the possibility of failure!

2 The approach has to be entrepreneurial not bureaucratic, decisive and with strong nerves.

3 Analyse precisely why the company is in trouble and build for tomorrow.

4 Be prepared to take risks, but always calculate and never leap in the dark.

5 Company management has to be professional throughout, with few short cuts.

6 Running a tight ship brings employees psychological, as well as financial, benefits.

7 The best possible managers have to be hired and motivated by their development potential.

8 Cash flow control is paramount, along with meaningful and detailed accounts.

9 The MD has to lead from the front and know enough to represent every facet of the company.

10 The MD (or a top director) has to lead marketing and be involved up to his neck.

11 Products must aim at clear markets, but avoid having all your eggs in one basket (market).

12 Product policy should balance current products that may be in decline, with the introduction of new products, enabling sales to be maintained and then increased with the transition.

13 The company's sales (product) appeal should be geared to goods or services sufficiently desirable over competitors, to carry a substantial margin.

14 R&D for new products, together with marketing costs, can be allowed to become a substantial overhead, so long as the margins are reasonably high.

15 For a smaller company, every market represents quite a large opportunity and venturing oversees multiplies the potential.

16 When success is verified by a profitable company no longer being so small, management philosophies and methods will have to change.

7

EMPLOYEES ALSO ENTREPRENEURS

Employees Also Entrepreneurs

Leading employees into entrepreneurial ways is a matter of personal attitudes, leadership and constant attention. If larger companies could infuse these principles throughout their many layers of management, relationships would be as good as in most smaller units. But even there, a professional approach is required and relationships can go sour, if attitudes at the top change. Company politics is a sure way to kill industrial relations at all levels. It can only be avoided by determination and open leadership from the top.

Remember that in a company, nothing stays secret for more than thirty seconds, especially bad news. Every unexplained new situation will lead to rumours of ghastly consequences. Whether a hold in production due to technical problems, or a spurt in stock building to anticipate an expected sales increase, the grass roots will interpret it as an impending redundancy. However confidentially one treats each employee's wage, any raise or anomaly will be widely known before it is entered into the computer. Nevertheless, everybody in the company must be regarded as an individual with personal hopes and fears, requiring nurturing, satisfying and sometimes prodding into action. Without adequate knowledge of company policies, if managers do not constantly seek to anticipate personnel problems arising from day to day activities, avoidable discontent will arise.

It will be said that in a smaller company, it should be easy to maintain good relationships with those at the coal face. Employees will regularly see the boss and being visibly in the same boat, will identify with the company's ambitions and its problems. Yet I have known the tiniest business with a complete lack of communication between proprietor and employee – as in the local hairdressing salon. Of course the answer boils down to people, their attitudes and their training.

The company from which I draw my example was not that small – about 120 in all. As smaller companies go, in many respects it was as complex to manage as those a hundred times larger. Its one advantage was the smaller number of layers from myself as the MD to the workstation. But its organisation was conventional, with "top team" managers respectively heading Finance, Sales, Engineering, Production and Quality Assurance. Each department broke down into functional sections and groups, leading to the coal face. Three distinct proprietary product groups required some fragmentation in design, production engineering and in manufacturing activity. Their differing market sectors and worldwide exports required a substantial multi-disciplined sales team, working direct and through a network of foreign distributors.

The disadvantage relative to larger companies was that in order to maintain innovation and timely deliveries to newly created markets, at a 40% p.a. growth rate, there were always great pressures on all concerned. Some of these were the creative ones of design and sales, others were those of costing and financial control required to produce the margins needed for growth without capital injections. While larger companies often have these types of pressure, the company's smallness did not allow specialist departments for planning, market research, legal problems, etc. All these had to be provided by entrepreneurial people wearing several hats. And the higher in the company, the more hats and the greater the pressures, leaving all with less time to think of anything but the job problems in hand.

My entrepreneurial organisation was predicated on delegation of responsibility to departmental managers, with suitably regular monitoring of their task progress and performance to ensure that nothing would fall between the cracks. While in most companies, such monitoring was normally pursued in monthly management meetings, in the pressure cooker environment of a fast moving small company, I chose mostly to hold one-on-one meetings with my managers. This combined the greater intensity of discussion that could be applied to a particular manager's sphere that is possible in such circumstances, with the freeing of other managers' time to get on with their jobs.

To keep the rest of the company fully informed and entrepreneurially motivated, annual company wide meetings were used to give all employees comprehensive information regarding products, markets, sales against budgets and much financial data. In formal presentations employing flip charts, employees were encouraged to question and to comment, with predictably motivating results.

So, this was more than a question of industrial relations? Firstly, since the company was too small to justify a personnel manager, even less a department, each departmental head was required to be his own personnel manager. To the extent it was necessary (mainly for the works manager), they were expected to keep abreast of statutory employment regulations and local practices. The company secretary, who was also the financial manager, took care of employee records, contracts of employment and pensions administration. But on the personal relationships front, it was each supervisor's clear duty to ensure good communications with his team. He was expected to inform, to motivate, to criticise and to discipline, as well as listen to shop floor ideas or grievances.

As a non unionised company, although there was a works council with formal monthly meetings, it was open discussion around work problems coupled with spare minutes on personal matters, which maintained a caring team spirit at all levels. The council ensured that each section of the factory was represented at a regular discussion chaired by the works manager. Formal minutes recorded the requests from the shop floor and progressed the agreed actions. I read these each month and sometimes attended the meetings. My personal involvement became far more instructive than a hundred reports and the works representatives really appreciated the opportunity to get at the boss direct. But it was perhaps the informal contact while discussing specific problems with designers, turners or salesmen which brought the two ends of the employee spectrum together in spirit. If the first or second line managers sometimes paid insufficient attention to their leadership roles, the irregular but not infrequent participation of the boss served to keep them up to it. At the same time, it provided opportunities for workers to put practical points at first hand.

The mixture of informality, with formal procedures in appropriate areas was as important as in a large company. Each employee knew his position in a formal job-grading scheme, which encompassed everybody. By insisting that managers produced job specifications and discussed these with their staff at salary review times, I could be reasonably assured that they were consciously objective with them about their performance. The grading bands provided for employees of differing calibres who were appropriately rewarded. They all fitted into a defensible pattern, which minimised anomalies. If an employee disagreed with his grading or salary, the manager had good reasons to offer for his assessment. Sometimes, the employee could show he was undervalued – for personal value or market reasons, when he would be re-graded and appropriately compensated.

Mutual trust and regard were taken for granted and so was fairness. So long as he first attempted to clear a grievance with his supervisor or manager, every employee could rely on a hearing in my office. On occasions, employees took their opportunity, but none tried to abuse it or to waste my time. The first time I was called "a fair man" by an employee was on one of the rare occasions when I had to sack somebody.

Generous conditions of service tended to be more than adequately repaid with loyalty and conscientious work. When staff conditions were first introduced on the shop floor, it needed some persuasion before all of the workers joined the excellent pension scheme. Although the contracts of employment only required the company to give pay during a limited period of sickness, depending on length or service, we always paid full salary until the worker was back in harness. Sometimes this went on for many months and only once was it necessary to discuss replacement with a man who was over-prone to long bouts of winter ailments. He also said I was a fair man and his sicknesses promptly reduced. They had more problems with the two-days sickness provision, when a doctor's certificate was not required. Mainly the women folk tended to suffer unexplained short illnesses with excessive regularity. This led to altering the rules (with works council agreement). Thereafter, only a maximum of two uncertified days of sickness in any month were paid and the women's health was soon greatly improved.

It pays to remember how important apparently small but sincere gestures can be to an employee. Visiting a laboratory technician who was leaving the company after long service, I noticed a memorandum pinned up over his bench. On inspection, I found it to be a note of congratulations on a job well done, that I had sent him several years earlier. I had completely forgotten about it, but the employee took it with him as a keepsake.

Flexibility of labour on the shop floor was absolute and it was common to switch people from a lightly loaded section to a busier one, doing completely different work. At a time of extreme pressure on production due to a subcontractor's default, the company required about three times its normal labour capacity. On putting the delivery problems and the consequent customer situation to the workforce, ready volunteers came forward, when I requested every unreasonable degree of help. The result was that a large proportion of (mainly married) female operators worked two daily shifts of six hours each, including Saturdays and Sundays for four and a half months. The truly entrepreneurial spirit was like Dunkirk, nobody was lost and the job was saved. The husbands apparently did the ironing.

Supervisory grades also pitched in, with the works manager, buyers and production engineers operating fly presses in the evenings. These members of the team would be invited to a presentation of the company's product and market policies, budgets and financial performance roughly once each year. They were expected to hold departmental meetings, to impart selected prime information to the workforce, but the top management liked to present the company position direct to the whole workforce from time to time and to answer questions in an open meeting. I learned a lot from these occasions and gained much respect for my workers' sincerity and for the sense behind some of their suggestions. At the same time, workers felt they were being treated as intelligent equals, colleagues rather than mere operators. Nevertheless, orders were orders and mutual respect ensured there was no indiscipline or undue griping.

The smallness of the company did not make the maintenance of good personnel relations any easier for top management. Up to twelve weeks per year of overseas travel on export business added to the many other calls on my time, leaving all too little time for personal contact in the factory. But I made a point of telling people where I had been and shared some of my optimism (and the customers' complaints) with employees at whatever level. The common workshop cynicism about overseas trips for directors was virtually absent, because workers identified such travel with results and with their future in the enterprise. Nothing made them more depressed than a quality problem, resulting in returned goods and they always pitched in with the post mortems, to find solutions regardless of who might have caused the problem.

Industrial relations can be poor in a small business too and it depends primarily on attitudes and on personalities. Everybody in the company should be encouraged to be an entrepreneur.

The main points

1. If employees are treated with equal respect and consideration, their loyalty follows.
2. Delegate responsibility to departmental managers, but monitor their performance.
3. Avoid large management meetings whenever one-on-one meetings can achieve more and save managers' precious time.
4. Keep all employees apprised of products, markets, sales, policies and finances. They will then positively identify with the company's policies and will make valuable suggestions.
5. When necessity for unreasonable efforts is candidly explained, employees behave like entrepreneurs.

8

CASE STUDY – INSOLVENCY TO TAKEOVER

TARGET

Case Study – Insolvency To Takeover Target

This account from my own real life experience of a company turnaround proves how an entrepreneur can not only overcome what appear to be impossible odds, but with intelligent management and enough energy, he can create a substantial profitable business, by pulling on his own bootstraps. It is the story of one memorable part of my entrepreneurial career.

Into a dog's breakfast

The Merchant Bank said, that although the company was losing money they expected it to break even by year's end. The incentive of a 10% share holding at nominal cost – and a guaranteed two-year contract – emboldened me to attempt a turnaround. Its chairman had led the company into its near terminal condition and would have to report to me as managing director! Not the best start for good relationships. Having come from a senior management position in a major electronics group, the first bad sign emerged during a visit for election to the board, a day or two before starting with the company. I needed £300 for the deposit on a company car, but the wages had not been paid and the cupboard was bare. The director from the Merchant Bank saved the day by putting in another £1,000, to follow their long series of monthly subsidies. I now had means of travelling to work.

More seminal signs showered down on my first day as MD, when the last financial year's audit arrived, showing that with 72 employees, sales had reached a bare £120,000 – and after necessary write offs for stock losses and R&D costs, the books showed a nearly equal loss of £110,000; quite an achievement, even at late 1960's rates. The main business in defence R&D and associated products was declining rapidly (courtesy of Harold Wilson's

Labour government) and first attempts to enter commercial markets were by means of a plethora of engineering projects pointing in every direction. The main customer for the only credible commercial product called to wish me well as the new MD – and to halt production of security sensors for his alarm systems. The Merchant Bank's loans at 10% interest were approaching £100,000 and the bank holding the current account was nervously continuing its £50,000 overdraft facility – on condition that the Merchant Bank loan was not called, and vice versa. A small company's workforce gets to know most of what is going on but rumours inevitably make perceptions much worse and seeing my arrival after several earlier new brooms, morale was correspondingly low. The only good news was the freehold on the ancient factory and labyrinthine office premises – and some good engineering talent, which needed leadership with coherent vision.

However, subject to producing a turnaround business plan during my first three months, I had a free hand. The chairman appeared to have accepted the restriction to forward looking R&D and keeping my back close to the wall, I was able to make a start. My brief introductory address gave everybody clear directions concerning their obligation to communicate all information that may affect any other employee or department. My first edict to the assembled managers was: "NO POLITICS!" – on pain of a quick demise. Nobody is indispensable." With that out of the way, I could begin to assess products and markets and investigate how things were being done.

Besides the now somewhat mired security sensors and an active torpedo fuze project for the Royal Navy, projects ranged from miniature boiler tube and even intra colonic cameras, ferrous metal crack detectors, mass vaccination jet injectors, heavy-landing indicators and runway water depth instruments through to a range of vibration protection switches for heavy machinery. With potentially greater market prospects in the difficult to crack automobile industry, prototypes of a safety switch to prevent crash fires had been shown to Triumph and Rover. All of these looked highly interesting to any engineer – but how many might find a profitable market?

With publicity help from the Board of Trade and the BBC World Service, export enquiries were piling up, but remained mainly unanswered, though some agents had been appointed – primarily for synergy with their defence related customers around Europe. However a crack detector was receiving enquiries from most corners of the globe and a London distributor was buying small quantities of the somewhat unreliable Jet Injector vaccination gun.

Mass vaccinations of the MD and his family

Mass vaccination by the W.H.O. as East Bengal becomes Bangladesh

A couple of engineers wearing sales hats cavalierly took material from the stores without proper recording and were without the leadership of a sales manager. The chief engineer and his team were overworked by the diversity of projects (at least between 9 and 5) and by their free run to interfere in the manufacturing process, over a protesting works manager's head. Fortunately, the defence business had necessitated formal quality assurance and inspection procedures, so records and a formal drawings library existed. The company secretary/accountant with two helpers produced monthly figures, which became one of my first priorities to understand. This was better done after delving into the factory and its costing records, besides getting to know the evidently competent workers and their machinery.

It didn't take many shop floor conversations to discover that most jobs were remade twice or more, as engineering changes leapfrogged with manufacturing – and even worse, nobody could verify the true cost of making anything. With an eye to keeping cash flowing, there had been no compunction about charging labour hours to the customer likely to pay the soonest and all in all, management was a veritable dog's breakfast. No wonder money was flowing out faster than the Merchant Bank could pump it in. Now by kicking our all too timid accountant hard enough and regularly enough to chase moneys due from customers, we could just about generate enough cash flow to get by between inputs from the Merchant Bank.

Early actions and planning

If the company was to grow into anything worth while, a properly constituted management structure would be essential, with totally independent manufacturing and engineering reporting to me, alongside professional accounting for accurate costing. Ideally, a strong sales manager should be recruited, but with such daily haemorrhage, for some time we would not be able to afford anything better than adding sales management to my duties. The Merchant Bank and the chairman's idea that such a small company only needed a bookkeeper and a "foreman in a bowler hat" had to be overcome and after some argument, I got my way. Besides separating out and clarifying the management lines of responsibility, to ensure that everybody knew what was going on, a daily Reader File of correspondence was circulated to all managers and above all, proper costing systems with realistic profit margins were laid down. Regular visits to the shop floor quickly dispelled the cynicisms seen on my first day and enthusiasm began to build, along with a constantly emphasized budgeting and cost saving culture.

The torpedo fuze manufacturing contract with the Admiralty promised a large chunk of our following year's sales, if the development of prototypes went to plan. This had to be a priority, even while private venture R&D emphasis would be directed to commercial product lines. The Crack Detector and the Jet Injector provided some revenue, but the emphasis soon crystallized towards Security and the Automobile Safety switches, with Vibration Protection Switches remaining "sink or swim" products taking minimal engineering priority. The business plan was coming together and despite the depths from which I was having to dig the company out, my enthusiasm burgeoned – and the work force followed closely behind.

Besides regular trips to the Continent, I began to join low cost overseas trade missions to the USA and to Japan, where many export leads were pointing. Once en route to Japan, the extra cost of adding other Far East destinations, Australia and back through the USA to a Board of Trade subsidized trip became minimal. Though such a tour took me away for five weeks, by carrying every production and delivery schedule as well as budgeted inward and outward cash flows in my briefcase, I was able to keep an eye and a firm hand on progress back at the ranch.

Between the USA and the Japan missions, we had persuaded Triumph to specify a fuel pump cut off crash switch on three sporty models, with deliveries to start in early 1969. Now the production engineering and tooling for volume manufacture using injection moulded plastics became the top priority. Not the familiar £600 torpedo fuzes to be carved out of solid metal in twos and sixes, but hundreds per day at prices nearer to £1 – with the same high degree of reliability and repeatability of performance. At the same time, improvements in the design of the security sensor and whole electronic systems to control the sensor outputs for alarm systems had to be developed. This would not only increase our revenues, but greatly increase the company's otherwise component-limited marketing clout. Small and unprofitable as the business still was, I budgeted the prime cost of R&D at 10% of expected sales revenues.

Knife in my back

Before leaving for Japan, I indicated that a further £5,000, or at most £10,000, would be needed from the Merchant Bank during my anticipated 5-week absence. This was agreed, but it was only at the furthest point from the UK that I received a call from our Merchant Bank director. In my absence, the chairman and our accountant had in their wisdom decided that the company needed an immediate £20,000 cash injection, they had cancelled the arrival of a much needed and just recruited works manager, fired my secretary and made a couple of dozen workers redundant! The stab in the back had long been coming. Nobody at the Merchant Bank or the factory seemed to know the complete figures, copies of which I took care to carry with me, nor exactly why this cash was "essential", yet they knew better. Reluctantly, I finished the trip, before racing home with high levels of interest gained from a major group in the US and many others – after which I refused to go back to the factory, until the Merchant Bank would decide whether to trust me or to trust the "old guard" that had led them to needing new management.

In my study at home I gritted my teeth, while clandestinely pursuing my USA contacts for a couple of weeks, before being invited to meet the managing director of the Merchant Bank and the company's agitated chairman, who totally failed to justify a raft of figures and accusations. The £20,000 injection was never taken up. Finally they decided to trust me – and the chairman was out – with a year's consulting contract enabling me to have him write a compendium of the technology he had originated, but never recorded. Now I had to give a final figure for the cash the company would need, before it would need no more – and putting this at £30,000 over the coming year, this amount was promised. Their parting words were, "You can have up to this amount and you have a totally free hand – but don't ask for any more money, because you won't get it!" The total debt was now a thumping nine times the value of the company's equity, but I went back with a will, to continue pulling the company up by its bootstraps.

Only by the bootstraps

After wastefully settling with the works manager who never came, search for an experienced and professional replacement was even more urgent and such ill afforded time consuming recruitment exercises continued to bug me, as better accounting managers also became necessary. "Perhaps it was me", I thought – but we went through half a dozen accountants in my time; some had integrity, fewer had acumen. I failed to find a single accountant with both acumen and integrity! How to tread the line between keeping people with valuable company experience and getting more capable replacements? Their real value would only become known perhaps six months after arrival, by when it would be too late if I had made an unfortunate choice. It was essential to find people willing to live a small company's more intensive life with less support than big organisations could offer. At the same time, to remain competitive with larger companies, we had to offer equally attractive salaries and conditions.

Delegation of as much responsibility as possible had to be a policy, tempered by regular monitoring of progress in each department. Weekly management meetings quickly gave way to bilateral meetings between myself and departmental managers, to maximise everybody's available time for their own job. At these weekly meetings, managers were expected to have met previously agreed benchmarks of progress, which I assiduously kept as reminders in my Day-Timer Diary, soon to be christened "his Black Book". The difficulty lay where managers were failing to meet their promises, or where they failed to motivate their staff proactively enough. In these circumstances, in a company that was picking itself up from the floor and could easily reverse into terminal failure again, I could not for a moment contemplate allowing a reversal to occur. Consequently where I saw inadequate performance, unless it became absolutely necessary to make a change by firing somebody, I would get sufficiently involved to compensate for whatever was lacking. This was not reneging on delegation; for on the other side of that coin, delegation is no excuse for top management to abrogate overall responsibility. In the final analysis, the Merchant Bank would hold me responsible and it would be my neck! My oft-repeated exhortation and message became:

> *"There is no such thing as failure. Don't tell me why something can't be done. Tell my how you will get it done. If you truly can't accomplish something, tell me before it's too late, what additional resources you need in order to get it done. Like circumventing the proverbial ten foot high wall, there is always a way to bypass it or get your leg over, if you apply appropriate tools and sufficient energy."*

By the end of my first financial year, we had delivered the torpedo fuze prototypes and won our £70,000 production contract – only to see the torpedo itself cancelled after we had made less than half of the units. With a lot of money committed for materials, we claimed compensation for termination and only after much governmental back-pedalling and brinkmanship on my part, we got £19,000. Nevertheless, the loss of this work led to making more people redundant, bringing our numbers down to thirty eight, the only time the job caused me any loss of sleep, yet those I had to sack understood and took it on the chin, while the remaining employees' efforts never waned. Still, with almost double the turnover employing half the original number of people, we roughly quadrupled productivity. Not yet quite at break even, but seemingly going in the right direction – and entirely without yet further cash injections.

Car crash switches in Italy

As car crash switch sales proliferated from Triumph to Jaguar, MG, Renault and later BMW, the company's Italian agent was purportedly negotiating a license agreement with Fiat. He kept it unusually close to his chest and when he would still not arrange for me to meet Fiat myself after several visits to Milan, he introduced a Baron, supposedly a friend of Fiat's chairman, Gianni Agnelli. That Agnelli would be bothered by such a small matter seemed unlikely, but I was assured, "All would be arranged". Yes and how! Soon they bluntly informed me that together, they would take two thirds of the license fees! In their flood of Italian invective, I had caught the name of the Fiat person with whom they were negotiating and at this point I walked out. With the help of the British Consul, I found and appointed a different agent and the Consul made an appointment for me at Fia . Contrary to the original drafts offering a fee and very low royalties, I negotiated higher royalties and full disclosure of Fiat's manufacturing techniques. They were ready to sign, when it transpired that Fiat had a problem with the company's patent, which at the request of our departed chairman, the recently fired agent had registered – in his own name. A half-year of litigation in Milan finally led to a settlement, literally on the court steps – we had our patent back – and Fiat had a license. In the automobile industry, we were now beginning to arrive. Ruefully I said, "If only my many visits to Detroit and Washington could also bear fruit."

Innovations in security

Our security portfolio had taken the desired turn from components to systems, but since our intruder detection was by sensing vibrations, the industry buyers and insurance companies wielding the power of accepting or denying specifications, determined that they would generate too many false alarms. Past vibration sensing systems had indeed been so plagued, but the company's discriminating technology avoided false alarms. Government departments were using our sensors for important installations ranging from building structures including the National Gallery to the Severn Bridge and to prison fences – but the technically ignorant alarm companies and insurance surveyors knew better. Factory demonstrations worked perfectly and still, specifications were turned down. Finally, I had my own home fitted with sensors on every window and every door and after some weeks passed without false alarms despite five rampaging teenagers, I began to demonstrate in a realistic and live environment. Now alarm engineers, insurance surveyors, major company directors, overseas agents, air marshals and other government officials made the pilgrimage to our home and aided by an endless supply of coffee and biscuits, slowly the message began to sink in. My articles appeared regularly in security magazines and the BBC broadcast a "Tomorrow's World" television feature about "The burglar proof house". The world began to believe we had a product.

Presentation of security innovations to industry and the press

My "lecture circuit" occupied many evenings to address groups of alarm company people and insurance surveyors. Always carrying a small demonstration sensor and electronic bleeper in my pocket, I lost no opportunity to demonstrate the capabilities of our sensor system at any function or party gathering to which I could gain access. Greatly amused, many eventual friends christened me "Mr. Inertia Switch". An artist among the British Insurers Association's surveyors created cartoons, that were published in the BIA's journal. Security shows would see the company's smallest booth of the industry inundated with local and overseas customers and representative agents vying to distribute the system, soon providing representation across Europe, the USA and Australia, with additions in the Far East and South Africa. Visits to these destinations began to add significant exports to the company's UK business and although crash fire safety switches were being sold in six figure quantifies for the lower volume cars, the security segment of the business soon overtook its turnover. Meanwhile, the "sink or swim" products continued to add income, with minimal call on engineering effort. My many overseas trips and the beginnings of establishing a significant export business came to the attention of senior figures at the Board of Trade, which I later discovered was the origin of our Buckingham Palace garden party invitation.

As nicknamed in the industry, 'Mr. Inertia Switch' in a cartoon

A new factory and interest arrears repaid, by developing property

Despite the weight of interest payments on our loans and the now happily necessary increases in personnel, we were beginning to see profits – if somewhat patchy. Employment was approaching one hundred and the factory "garret" was bursting at the seams; we just had to find new premises. A Council road project was planned to drive straight through the factory, leading to the welcome possibility of compulsory purchase at a valuation of £46,000, well over the mortgage and the book values. Soon after we started searching seriously, the Council changed its mind about the road and a local builder with adjoining property made an offer well below the modest Council valuation. A frequent visitor, the builder would not raise his offer and in the early '70s period of building boom, I began to look at the potential development value of the site. Before long, I was convinced that with planning permission for three floors of offices and parking on our quarter acre, obtainable rents would value the site at up to £100,000. It took another year of disappointments before I convinced a developer to buy the site and the whole row of shops beyond for just such a development and after various joint development profits formulae, we agreed on a fixed £70,000. On hearing he had competition, the builder swiftly raised his offer to match this – but he was sent away with a flea in his ear.

The current company secretary found a modern factory six miles West along the A30, for which we agreed a fourteen year lease, allowing us to use the proceeds of the sale to create a customised factory and office complex with double our previous space. For the first time in history, the company had no overdraft – until it repaid over £30,000 of accumulated interest owing to the Merchant Bank. Starting Friday mid day, we accomplished the move over a weekend, production recommencing by midday on the Monday. Many people lost a lot of hair in the process, but they were in modern premises with room to expand. A minibus driven by factory personnel shuttled workers to the new premises and it also served to deliver products.

By the end of my fifth year, though the original defence business had been whittled right down, the new commercial business had more than tripled overall sales – which were rising increasingly, through 20-40% annually. Travelling frequently around Europe, to the US several times a year and occasionally to Australia, with a professional sales manager also hired, our marketing overhead became a significant 10% of sales, but still our margins were kept high enough to manage without any further cash from the Merchant Bank or from anywhere else. Perhaps we were now "on a roll". Nevertheless, in its timid wisdom after its investment became secure, the Merchant Bank's biggest worry was that I would ask for cash to sustain this healthy growth. Nothing was further from my mind, since we had become completely accustomed to the bootstrap process. However, they began to lean on me to find another shareholder who would help restructure the balance sheet and take a majority interest, leaving the Merchant Bank with no more than 25%. The Merchant Bank board member insisted, "you are the company's best salesman and only you can do it".

Hyper inflation and finding unnecessary investors

Now, in addition to stimulating and contributing to engineering efforts, sales trips around the UK and Europe, making sure that manufacturing coordinated with costing/accounting, overseeing pricing policy, starting new job grading and suggestion bonus schemes, maintaining the lenders' confidence, writing and lecturing – in between the longer overseas trips, I was supposed to look for potential investors. Needless to say, my priorities remained on the main job and far from being relaxed, they had to be ramped up as the company developed. Whenever possible, I showed potential partners around the company and its still unhealthy, if improving books.

Near hyperinflation during the Heath government and the "three day week" engendered by a miners' strike had costs soaring. Bought out materials, the largest part of factory cost leapt week by week, along with the $800 per ounce price of gold, which dominated the security sensors' cost. Labour costs also rose, but somehow we managed to keep running without requiring more loans. To the amazement of our accountant with none too much acumen, I made an in-depth analysis of the company's costs and showed that had the UK's rate of inflation been "only" double that in West Germany, the company would have an additional £90,000 of cash. This would have been almost enough to pay off the Merchant Bank's entire loan, saving £9,000 of annual interest – a very significant addition to profit! Like many companies, our output did not suffer from the three day week – though we worked it to the last available night and day minute.

In America, car crash switches, "a cure for which there is no ill"

Resulting from the Fiat relationship, we had test results showing that crash fires are only likely to occur if electric sparks or short circuits ignite fuel vapour. We therefore built prototypes of a heavy-duty crash switch that would disconnect the car's battery and also the alternator, so that a crash would remove all possible electrical ignition sources. Fiat bought and road tested a thousand pre-production models satisfactorily, after which we added a means of automatically turning on fused safety circuits such as hazard flashers, at the same time as cutting ignition sources. Called by Jaguar's technical director "your most luxurious model", its safety effect eclipsed the simpler fuel pump cut off switches so far used by the auto manufacturers, though it cost about £1 or so more – not a lot compared with the cost of building a Jaguar. He ordered this model for production and tooling was well advanced, when in an economy campaign, the technical director was overruled by his MD – the same Geoffrey Robinson, who in recent times went in and out of Tony Blair's government! Jaguar finished up using the same fuel cut off switch as all others. This would have repercussions for our attempts in America.

Detroit executives' unanimous 1970's perceptions that "you guys in England are always on strike" were countered with evidence, that the smaller companies like this one had zero problems with trade unions. Nevertheless, they remained unanimously sceptical about crash switches and though GM, Ford, Chrysler and American Motors gave me courteous hearings, while I pursued licensing prospects with Bendix and others, it was clear that none of them would specify an inertia crash switch unless it was mandated by safety legislation. In Washington, the Department of Transportation's National Highway Traffic Safety Administration – colloquially known as "NITSA" – had mandated a Fuel Systems Integrity standard and was sympathetic to my arguments for a similar *Electrical* Systems Integrity standard. But this would only be considered if a cost benefit could be proved. In my "spare time" I collected what test evidence and sparse accident statistics existed, then coupling these with NITSA's societal costs for deaths and serious injuries, I used the most conservative of the figures to arrive at an annual societal cost of $300m – against $30m to supply every production car in the USA with our "most luxurious model". Next thing was a purchase order for a small number of crash switches from a testing organisation in Arizona. This soon proved to involve comprehensive laboratory tests of how fuel vapour could and could not be ignited, followed by eight full-scale car crash tests using the company's inertia switches. Firstly four crashes were arranged to guarantee a crash fire, then four crashes in identical conditions used the Electrical Cut Off switch. None of these caught fire. The subsequent DOT report confirmed my arguments virtually chapter and verse and their film of the tests contained dramatic footage in a split screen, showing the identical crashes – one above without fire and below it, a massive conflagration. The commentator's narrative concluded, "Which car would you prefer to be driving?" Soon, NITSA issued an "Advance Notice of Proposed Rule Making", the effect of which would mandate the company's solution – bringing it to the brink of its best ambitions.

But still not enough to move Detroit! Calling inertia switches a "cure for which there is no ill", without exception, the motor companies poured cold water on the test conclusions, adding totally spurious assertions that crash switches would cause road hazards, due to false activations leaving cars dangerously scattered on highways, without power. All my revisiting, re-presenting of data and exhortations fell on deaf ears, while the upcoming 1975 US general election finally paralysed NITSA, which did no more about the prevention of crash fires. The film proved a powerful selling tool, which was used widely with European car manufacturers – the Italians mouthing deep suspicions that the company had bribed somebody to produce such results!

Perimeter security developments and a new systems company

Meanwhile, the security sensing systems now with a well known brand name continued their worldwide sales growth, by then aided not only by my own repeated travels but also a sales manager's and his team pursuing areas I had opened up. Following experimentation on our back garden fence and many tests and demonstrations, a big additional market was opening up for the system to detect intruders cutting through or climbing over chain link and similar perimeter fences. Even more was it necessary to overcome universal scepticism and disbelief, ruining many pairs of my shoes in demonstrations. However, with the company's and the system's widely accepted credibility, it began to catch on both at home and in export markets. With a little ingenuity, our engineers designed logic circuits I had specified, that would tolerate kids kicking footballs against a protected fence without causing false alarms, yet it would detect anybody climbing over it. No competitor could match this performance even at higher cost, so though we still had to convince every prospect one at a time, sales rose t[illegible]ere the company was eventually selling systems to protect one hundred miles of perimeter fences per year. Still a small business, but making a definite worldwide mark in the security industry.

UK government departments which had been the earliest users of inertia sensors became disenchanted with the quality and the cost of services provided by the big companies. The Ministry of Public Buildings & Works approached us, to design and install a complete security system against potential sabotage of a big dam, involving products we would have to obtain and integrate with their own. This was encroaching on customer territory and after treading carefully, I established a subsidiary with a wall of confidentiality to protect against perceptions that they may have created a conflict of interest. The system was successfully installed at a fraction of the cost from the "big boys" and enabled me to start building an independent systems business within a developing group of companies. A totally different business of contracting for large projects as opposed to manufacturing, we recruited an experienced manager and project engineers capable of bidding and profitably executing such projects with reliability. Our motor was running ever faster and my time was spread ever more thinly. The work of this systems part of the group extended to contracts in the Middle East and with NATO, besides London's World Trade Centre built by Taylor Woodrow and at the smaller end, the private home of a recently retired RAF Air Marshal. Each project was won in open competition and with its own difficulties and peculiarities.

Initially to avoid all contacts with our customers being of the "adversarial" selling kind, the company took membership of the British Security Industries Association, which enabled me to sit on committees debating standards and practices. Widely perceived as a company of high integrity that pulled its weight in innovation and exports, it was now possible to establish relationships of a more equal kind and further widen the company's credibility and clout. In a few years this credibility lead the BSIA to elect me to its council and to chair its Manufacturers Section. The flywheel continued to accelerate – totally on self-generated cash.

A US joint venture for the security market

The compelling yet elusive plum remained the US market, as the stamps in my passport bore evidence. The big players in the US security market were as hard to crack as the auto companies. It seemed that we would only have to get ADT or Honeywell widely specifying our security system and they would expand exponentially. After an initial agreement in Virginia, which got nowhere and eventually led to the development of a competitive sensor, I established distribution by a smaller manufacturer in California. Gradual success relied on piecemeal sales to the big companies' branches and to the many smaller security installers, before this distributor could make much impression. To get their priorities moved somewhat from their own products onto distributing ours, the distributor's motivation had to be greatly increased and I proposed a joint venture company. Much against conventional wisdom received from all around, I made this a 50/50 arrangement. We sent an experienced sales engineer to California with his family and put him under the management of the US side of the venture. Two directors from each side constituted the board, with a rotating chairmanship. To protect against the possibility of the company's largest market being frittered away by any management failures on the US side, we retained a veto on the general manager appointment and on marketing strategy. It took some hair pulling before there was agreement, but it transformed the distribution effort and sales began to rise. The company put very little cash in and after creating detailed business plans and payback forecasts to satisfy the bureaucracy, significantly more went in with the aid of the currently available Market Entry Guarantee Scheme offered by the British Overseas Trade Board. Now there was a quasi US company better able to sell to both commercial and to US Government agencies. As a result among many other projects, Andrews Air Force Base housing the US President's Air Force One was still protected by the company's security system many years later.

American auto industry breakthrough and final success

More than ten years into the "turnaround", despite significant business with European car manufacturers and profitable sales, the Merchant Bank and others on the company's board opposed my efforts to pursue the auto market, on the grounds of excessive cost for R&D and quality assurance and supposedly minimal margins they might earn. At virtually no extra cost during visits to the USA on security industry business, I nevertheless persevered towards that elusive breakthrough.

Hitherto vain attempts to sell crash switches into America now received an unexpected fillip. A Ford Pinto had caught fire in a rear end crash and the resulting Court judgment awarded damages of $107m against the Ford Motor Company. Henry Ford II had given me contacts in the company before and I wrote a succinct letter offering my sympathies, but advising that if Ford only followed some of the company's European customers which used crash switches, he may avoid such a contingency. That won his attention and Ford's Chief of Vehicle Design soon wrote inviting a visit. Wasting no time, I arrived at the Design Chief's office – who had just come from seeing Henry Ford and mainly questioned matters relating to quality control and general integrity. With defence level quality assurance well enshrined, these seemed satisfactory and he was next sent to the Purchasing Director, who had also just come from seeing Henry Ford. An official inquiry quickly followed and after a series of engineering visits in both directions and negotiations with several levels of Ford Purchasing, we received the first order to supply for the 1980 model year's larger vehicles. As with Jaguar eight years back, to save the odd Buck they took the least cost fuel pump cut off switch, instead of the more effective Electric Cut Off "most luxurious model". But now the biggest door on earth was wide open and Ford's main entrance lobby display of "Quality One Suppliers" came to show the company, as its first non-American recipient of that award. I was more than willing to be thankful for "small" mercies.

With the addition of initially modest quantities for Ford and the burgeoning 40% growth of the security business including the 60% due to the now established export business, sales were running at twenty times those when I first started. The acquisition of another small security sensor manufacturer had made us into a group of three operating companies and at last, we were profitable and paying dividends. The balance sheet had been straightened out a few years earlier, with the entry of a new majority shareholder and conversion of outstanding debt into equity. However up to the current time, the new investor's expenses taken from the company grossly exceeded his input for the equity, so even by 1980, *we had maintained our growth – effectively without any outside cash*. While the rate of this uphill grind by boot straps to success may be eclipsed by other examples of growth, the Group's subsequent rate of expansion and its profitability were clearly based on the foundations laid during its emergence from a very deep pit.

In the four years following the first Ford contract, quantities rose to an annual rate of three million units and the profits multiplied correspondingly, to the point where the company was sold for £6m. Then, as quantities continued to climb still further, the company went public and subsequently, every Ford car carried the crash switch. That business remained the company's main profit earner for twenty years. Many newer products supplied to other auto industry customers produced total annual revenues in the £160m range. Before the market slide from the "dot.com" boom, total capitalisation reached £500m and remained comparably consistent with the stock market. The company was sold to Honeywell in 2004 – for £207m in cash! Not a bad result after nothing but bootstraps until the company's floatation.

What does this case study teach us?

1 An MD's full authority and freedom are necessary, for the speedy measures required.
2 With total dedication, persistence and stamina, it is possible to dig a failing company out of the deepest hole.
3 First, analyse exactly why it is failing and get to know the employees.
4 Make a business plan – and be prepared to adjust it in the light of events.
5 Inculcate a culture of never contemplating failure.
6 Create the culture of cost control among all employees, including the little savings.
7 Listen to employees' suggestions from the coal face and take them seriously.
8 Cash flow controls above all – including robust collection from customers.
9 Employ strict, accrual accounting practices and cost controls.
10 Configure management structure for growth, to suit the company's future needs.
11 Define and refine market needs, using your intimate personal contact with it.
12 Concentrate on the main products, while others sink or swim without distracting effort.
13 Develop products to match market needs and don't stint on R&D.
14 Look to products with sufficient innovation, to see off any competition – and build in healthy margins.
15 Exports and new markets can multiply a small company's sales and its growth prospects.
16 Offer professional analyses to make the arguments for a groundbreaking product's market credibility.
17 Sceptical markets can be won over to adopt even if in reality, there is a "the cure for which there is no ill" logical need in the market. But it takes time.
18 Keep obsolescent products that contribute to the bottom line just long enough for new high-margin products to take over.
19 You should lead from the front in marketing and selling, while also keeping close to product development.
20 Insist on zero company politics and on full communication – up/down and laterally.
21 Require managers to meet budgets and timescales, allowing few excuses. "Don't tell me you cannot do it, work out how you could do it – or ask for any additional resources you need to get the job done."
22 Generous interpretation of workplace rules and treating employees as equals brings loyalty and willingness to make huge efforts.
23 Capital expenditure can often quickly create much greater operating savings.
24 Never undersell the company – particularly to a potential buyer.
25 Keep fit enough, to sustain a punishing work schedule.

9

ENTREPRENEURISM IN LARGE COMPANIES

Entrepreneurism In Large Companies

Latent entrepreneurism was beginning to show its face in my psyche, when my experience had still been solely in a large and somewhat bureaucratic aircraft company. Perhaps I did not realise this and when deciding to make a career move into marketing, I obtained three good job offers just before being sent on a brief visit to the USA, when I was able to visit Litton Industries to check on their inertial navigation equipment I had recently proposed for a UK project. After much questioning and rigorous inspection of this company's facilities, I was favourably impressed with their engineers' perceptible business acumen, as well as with the quality of the company's engineering and its results with high technology products in the field. On taking my leave, I felt obliged to tell my hosts that if the project went ahead, somebody else from my company in England would become their new contact, since I was about to leave for another job.

A heavy, but friendly hand promptly descended onto my shoulder and I was quickly propelled into the general manager's office, where I was immediately offered a job. This could either be in this rapidly developing company's main facility in California, its manufacturing facility in Hamburg or to start a new operation in London. The latter lone position would be a major challenge, to establish business in the UK while reporting only to directors in Switzerland and in the USA. This would be a really big leap from comfortable immersion within an organisation, into the task of creating an entirely new line of sales into a hostile and unreceptive market, with the minimum of help or supervision from distant management. Despite the odds against success, with the desire to cut my teeth in the commercial world, I felt compelled and accepted the challenge, in preference to any of the other offers.

The problem of fighting a hostile "City Hall"

My new employer was widely acknowledged as world leader in the avionics for navigating military aircraft – from attack fighters to long-range air transports. The UK's long and proud history of comparable developments included many successful aircraft projects, but in this field it was evidently a generation behind. The Government procurement ministries were pushing hard in supporting British industry to develop indigenous products and contracted with several UK firms to develop their equipments for Royal Air Force and Royal Navy projects. However, the RAF itself was not satisfied that their Operational Requirements (O.R.) would be met by these still putative developments, especially within their desired time scales. Knowing about the more advanced US systems already in service and of the early, untested state of the UK developments sponsored by the procurement ministries, the RAF's O.R. officers were sympathetic towards serious consideration of US equipment and this gave this "new boy" entrepreneur and his US employer some grounds for hope.

However, with the Ministry's entrenched policies and contract commitments with favoured suppliers to develop from scratch, it was clear that selling the US equipment would be a very uphill task. Entrepreneurism does not have to compete with patriotism and it became clear that in order to have any chance to sell against such a climate of resistance, it would be necessary to have the equipment manufactured in the UK and that the superior technology would also have to be made as available to UK industry and to the RAF, as if it had been developed by a British company. Now as the American company's UK manager, in my one-man London office I had to develop two strings to my attack bow – firstly to convince both the manufacturers of the aircraft into which my American equipment was proposed and the Ministry which was to procure for them, that our proposals were truly capable of serving the RAF's needs. Secondly, I would have to forge strong relationships between my US employer and British companies, which would finally build, supply and support the equipment – either in a joint venture, or under a license agreement giving full disclosure of the technology. This would mean dealing with major British companies at board level and newly nascent from a big company cocoon, at the age of thirty three I was being catapulted into an unfamiliar stratosphere and left very much to myself.

Getting down to work

After initial introductions by my immediate boss in Zurich, I was soon able to gain access to senior Ministry officials, the RAF's O.R. officers and a few of the personalities in British industry, where relationships might be explored. Now it was time to offer proposals for specific projects, whose complexity required considerable input from engineers in California, to produce the detailed specifications, test data and anticipated performance in the aircraft for which the systems were to be offered. This involved making visits to California and conversely, visits by engineers from there, bearing heavy manuals and sample equipment for presentations in England. It was also time to prepare the ground, by establishing a relationship within British industry.

With its open mind and relatively open doors to accredited and security-cleared people, The RAF's O.R. officers detailed its requirements sufficiently to enable Litton to be briefed and a proposal created. This was for an Inertial Navigation system, developing from its already operational systems in NATO's 1,000 F-104 fighters, whose in-service performance was a matter of record. The new system of even greater accuracy and lighter weight was already through its laboratory tests and into its own flight test programme, with encouraging results. An airplane being developed by the great Hawker Aircraft was a supersonic version of the Harrier jump jet, which required such a navigation system and the RAF was keen to get its hands on a system that would be ready on time. They preferred to back this proposal, rather than await the uncertain outcome of developments by companies in the UK.

However the Ministry already had a large investment in such developments and while it would always give me time of day to meet officials at levels through assistant directors, directors up to controller and would never say "never", it rarely volunteered helpful information and like a spider in its web, it sat in the middle sucking in information, without giving much out. Now was the time for approaches to be made by UK companies in a position to manufacture the system, with Litton largely in the background.

A long UK-assimilated American, Harvey Schwarz was managing director of Britain's Decca Navigator with considerable successes in radar based navigation systems, Doppler Navigation systems for measuring aircraft ground speed and in "moving map" displays. These systems were entirely complementary to the Inertial Navigation system being offered and with its own technical development and manufacturing facilities, Decca Navigator was a highly credible partner for manufacturing the American system. Over some weeks, I established a strong relationship with Schwarz and his managers, leading to the configuration of a joint venture company to be established in the London area. I produced a suitable contract draft and negotiations of a joint venture agreement proceeded to the point where Harvey's boss, Decca chairman Sir Edward Lewis, invited Roy Ash, the president of Litton to London for finalisation of a Letter of Intent. The meeting duly took place, with me and my Decca counterpart orchestrating the top company officers through the details – until the two great men shook hands on a deal. So far so good – surprisingly smooth sailing for a novice entrepreneur acting as the lone UK manager. The Ministry was carefully kept informed and sat on the sidelines, inscrutably keeping its own counsel.

Equally vital would be to achieve the acceptance of the proposed system by the designers of the Hawker airplane. Besides the usual technical problems associated with the complex integration of electronic equipment into an aircraft's design and test programmes, there was one most important obstacle. Legendary designer and director Sir Sidney Camm was in charge of the supersonic jump jet – and he hated electronics – as he also hated Americans. To sell American electronics onto his airplanes was like trying to sell poison pills to a sabre-toothed tiger.

Fortunately, we received assistance from a former colleague of Camm acting as a consultant and with his help, managed to gain access to him. After some terse telephone conversations in trying to arrange for presentation of the proposals by visiting vice presidents from California, Camm truculently agreed to a date. "And what is that jamboree you want in the afternoon?" he demanded, concerning the high level presentation proposed after a first meeting with the working level engineers. Eventually the day arrived and the US top brass checked into a London hotel, leaving the vital equipment there during the morning, to avoid over pressurising a sensitive Camm. The great man came into the morning meeting unexpectedly and after a few minutes declaimed, "Well, why wait till the afternoon? Let's get on with the equipment demonstration now." With the equipment deliberately left in London, it took a lot of frantic telephone calling and expensive taxi rides from London to Kingston before a presentation could be mounted – giving Camm an excuse for further decrying American "inefficiency"! However, the ice had been broken and working level discussions continued towards the integration of the equipment into Camm's airplane.

In the meantime, the Decca deal was suddenly put into reverse by a competitor of Litton, who convinced Lewis that it would be too costly and risky for Decca to try manufacturing the Inertial Navigation equipment. Lewis opted out of the final signing meeting already arranged to be in California and sent Schwarz to explain. I got wind of this from my Decca counterpart and after spending a day on the telephone monitoring Schwarz's flight to Los Angeles, also took a flight there and attended what became a most friendly meeting and dinner of transatlantic top brass – without the desired outcome. On my return to London, I called Roy Ash to discuss possible deal saving tactics and Ash did exactly as advised – but the deal was dead.

Now, particularly since Hawker was part of the bigger Hawker-Siddely Group, I approached another Group member, DeHavilland, whose Weapons Department was equally suitable as a UK manufacturer and another relationship gradually built. Proposals to the Ministry to supply the American system now came from DeHavilland. Was this to be another match made in Heaven? Not if Sir Sidney Camm could help it!

The Royal Navy now had a project, to upgrade the Buccaneer aircraft with inertial navigation and I was quickly on the ball. Having met the Admiralty's equivalent officers to the RAF's O.R. branch and received details of the requirement, I was able to approach the Ministry, with a view to adding my proposal to those of four UK competitors who had been offered paid contracts to make proposals. Under a separate Ministry contract, the proposals were to be evaluated by Blackburn Aircraft, makers of the Buccaneer. In true entrepreneurial fashion, I enlisted assistance from colleagues in the US and Europe to produce an unsolicited proposal and went with a colleague to Brough in Yorkshire, where it was presented to Blackburn chief designer John Stamper. Stamper professed to be much impressed and promised to report his views to the Ministry, alongside the four paid proposal evaluations. It was not long afterwards, that the result became known – Stamper had selected the unsolicited US proposal over the four paid offers.

Surely, this was the breakthrough? Hotfoot, my director visiting from Zurich and I went to the Ministry, where we expected to negotiate a contract for commencing the project, based on Blackburn's selection. The PSO (Principal Scientific Officer) handling the project just below assistant director level met me with a deep frown and clear anger on his face. A Scot, who now revealed his absolute refusal to allow mere fair competition to interfere with his prejudices, McDuff had no intention of getting down to business. "This selection procedure is most unfair and you have not heard the last of this. I want the contract to go to a company in Scotland. Their design is moving along very well." In the Civil Service it appeared that none of the more senior directors or even higher would gainsay the recommendation of their main technical level PSOs. Decisions are hard enough to make at the best of times, but in any contentious situation, to overrule a PSO and be seen to make any misjudgement would risk a black mark on their reputation. I went up the chain and was received by every level up to the controller, with friendly but empty assurances of always being objective, etc. Thus, the relatively lowly PSO was the most powerful person in the chain and nothing was evidently done to curb his Scottish fervour.

In Stanmore, The General Electric Company (GEC) became my third attempt at creating a UK supply capability. Most sympathetic and quite enthusiastic to become the UK source for the American inertial navigation equipment, the directors set to and produced proposals to Hawker and the Ministry, for the ongoing supersonic Harrier development. I had got to know the Air Minister of the day, Hugh Fraser, and on incidentally meeting him in a different context, I was gratified to be asked, "Has your company received the official Request to Tender yet?" So at last, we need not rely on an unsolicited bid.

The bid was assembled with much work and calculation of costs, for GEC to present performance figures and prices for prototypes, pre-production models and first batch production systems over the required time scale. A multi-million pound bid, pencils were sharpened to give the RAF the best possible deal, with the reliable knowledge that their performance requirements would be comfortably met. No other competitor had equipment flying that was remotely comparable. They all required long development periods and considerable funding by the taxpayer. The US equipment would be UK built, the technology would be fully transferred via Litton's Canadian subsidiary, which was already supplying equipment to the Royal Canadian Air Force, and the country's capability in inertial navigation would leap a generation, without cost to the country.

A few weeks later the RAF's O.R. branch sat down with me for a friendly meeting. "We should tell you straight. The Ministry just submitted its conclusions and doubled your navigation error figures to 'include a transatlantic funk factor'. They also increased your price quote by almost double, to allow for more 'transatlantic factors' they consider necessary, making sure that your price would appear to be higher than your competitors. We are highly dissatisfied by all this and protests have gone up the Chief of Operational Requirements – and we believe to the Prime Minster. But don't hold out too much hope that you will get the job – that is if the airplane ever gets the go-ahead."

As it transpired, the aircraft itself was cancelled before it might have flown with any navigation equipment. Instead, the Ministry ordered a US fighter, the F-4 Phantom, which went into RAF service. Although it was a highly used aircraft by the USAF and required no special development, its engines were replaced by British jet engines. Here the UK was not behind US technology and although a lot of cost was involved in adapting the aircraft to a different engine, the decision to use British here was understandable.

The US Air Force's Phantoms also flew with inertial navigation systems made by Litton. Four hundred such aircraft were in service and I made proposals to use the same system, but manufactured in the UK. This failed to sway McDuff and the British Phantoms were specified with the Scottish inertial navigation system.

After three years of earnest effort, largely on my own against the entire weight of UK based competition, which had close Ministry relations and ongoing contracts, after three successive partnership prospects for UK manufacturing had fallen onto barren ground, I got the message. This project was never going to fly – unless perhaps Litton and one of the UK prospects would make the risky investment of actually starting a fully functional company, before any contract prospect could be reasonably certain. Unsurprisingly, neither the US nor the UK companies were prepared to take such a risk. At that point, I decided that enough was enough. I was offered and accepted a senior management position by one of the three companies I had turned down three years earlier – at double the originally offered salary.

Four years later after the Phantom was in RAF service, I hosted an informal lunch with the Ministry's Controller and the RAF's Air Commodore for Operational Requirements. Notwithstanding the disappointments of the past, our personal relationship had been established and remained friendly. I asked them innocently, "How is the Scottish system working out in the Phantom?" After exchanging glances, the Controller replied, "It is still not working". I then asked, "How is McDuff doing nowadays? "Oh, he has retired from the Civil Service", they answered. "He now works for that Scottish company."

Lessons to be learned

1 Some large companies are willing to encourage and support entrepreneurism. So long as the personalities, the company's culture and the vibrations look good, it is worth taking the plunge.

2 Never fear being in at the deep end and rising to an apparently impossible challenge.

3 With sufficient common sense and clearly established integrity, one can negotiate with big organisations, all the way from working level to the main board.

4 Don't be afraid to push the boundaries and don't lightly take "No" for an answer.

5 Don't expect more honesty and integrity from Civil Servants, than from any other parts of society.

6 There comes a time, when the best of efforts and resources become unequal to a situation.

7 Don't burn any bridges. Just always keep your head – and be sure to fall on your feet.

10

MEASURES OF SUCCESS

Measures Of Success

Strictly speaking, an entrepreneur can hardly know whether or not his efforts are successful, until he sells out or goes public. Even the latter can be an illusory or temporary indication, unless his success is measurable in purely personal terms, as it may be if he takes his bag of gold at the time of a sale or a floatation.

The big problem with some investors is that they do not always appreciate the potential of a small, growing business, unless and until it is blatantly evident from the dividends they receive. Taking a long-term business view, making dividend distributions could be a sure way to deny such a company its growth funds. If the responsibility for nurturing a modest venture capital investment is given to a junior executive, not long out of business school, he may suffer from delusions of grandeur. The short term returns from his portfolio which might quite wrongly earn the feathers in his cap at the institution's year end, sometimes blinds such studs to the capital profits which would be earned by selling the investment at the right time, a few years ahead.

My smallish enterprise suffered repeated criticisms for patchy profits, although it was growing healthily and rapidly, entirely on self-generated cash flow. The growth was achieved by the creation of new products and expanding markets, by my company's in-house research and development, coupled with aggressive international sales promotion. The company had gained a high reputation in its market sectors and overseas distributors hammered on the door, yet our investor's "Guardian Angel" would only quote his textbooks and lament the lack of dividends and the fear of being asked for cash. At board meetings, apart from boilerplate references to ratios and the control of stocks or debtors, he could barely contribute towards the practical decisions to be taken about products, manufacturing, pricing or market strategy. His superiors were busy with deals worth orders of magnitude more than their equity in our company and he mainly remained silent, seeming only to understand ratios and short-term results.

An entrepreneurial business may require significant overheads for R&D and for quality assurance procedures in an industry where margins could become tight. Where new technology has continued to lead an ever more receptive market with virtually no direct competition, the fact can completely escape the Guardian Angel's attention. Maintaining a course, pursuing large volumes and profit down the road, he would mainly earn us institutional scorn.

Investors' perceptions can be so blinkered, that despite their investee generating sufficient profits to pay modest dividends while maintaining the growth rate without cash injections, they continue to value the company at a bare liquidation level. In one case in which I was intimately concerned, the institution finally sold its 25% holding to the principal shareholder for a paltry sum, after strong indications of the company's worth being five times higher became evident from outside offers.

The measure of success in a privately held company remains somewhat subjective, until an acid test can prove the true value of past business judgements. Macroeconomics as well as changes in localised market conditions can often determine the degree of success, despite the quality of management and business judgements applied by the entrepreneur. Nevertheless, absolute measures of share value can be gleaned from a number of practical criteria and can provide pointers, besides the natural measures of profitability ratios and growth regularly documented in the management media.

A successful acquisition is surely more likely, if the business under consideration is evaluated in greater depth, than is possible by even the most experienced investigations of its balance sheet. Such an evaluation is best made by people who have held line responsibility for running a comparable business, with all the implied planning, problem solving, general management and entrepreneurial risk taking involved. Those financial analysts, professional investors and consultants, whose management experience has been mainly peripheral can miss the cardinal points, when analysing performance from pieces of paper.

Whether it is a manufacturing or a service business, it is a company's people, top and middle level managements coupled with its variously skilled employees, who will firstly determine its future prospects. There are many relatively intangible questions, which make for a company's actual or potential success. In analysing the prospects, the practiced entrepreneur-investor will look for these as well as for the figures.

Is there clear, strong leadership from the top and is there a team spirit among the top executives? Are they open to constructive criticism or do they snipe and score off each other? Are they visibly enthusiastic and proud of their company? Do they have a clearly defined set of company goals in constant view and do they willingly use these as their main daily incentive?

In larger companies, middle management can be the Achilles heel, if they are not in tune with top management or if they feel unable to lead their departments with effective authority. In smaller companies, the difficulty may be in the finding of highly motivated middle managers, if there appear to be more avenues for promotion in larger corporations. Yet the team spirit and job satisfaction in a well led smaller company can retain and continue to motivate such managers for years and an experienced eye can detect which situation prevails.

- Are there clearly defined responsibilities and communication patterns throughout the company?

- Does everybody know how he can best contribute his time and his skills to help attain the company goals and is there an impression of purposeful hustle and bustle, as one walks and talks through the company's operations?

- Is the labour force part of the team and does it regard itself so?
- Does the whole company receive regular information about its objectives, problems and its performance, or is there a "we and they" attitude?
- Is there a quality problem with products or service?

If there is, it is likely that this coal face measure of success points to a management problem somewhere in the company.

Before evaluating a company in this depth, it goes almost without saying, that the basic accounting figures have already been checked, with reasonably favourable results. But these only point to the past. What of the future? A highly profitable company can be on the verge of an abyss, while an apparently poor financial performer is sometimes rejected without realisation of its imminent potential.

For an investor to achieve a return which is more than a transient promise, he must choose a company with more than the superficial measures of success.

Yes, the performance today must be essentially sound, with realistic potential for sufficient profits to produce a growing asset. The real assets of a company may be nowhere to be found in the balance sheet. But they can exist in very real terms, to arrive on the balance sheet at a later date. Then, they may prove to be much more valuable than the commonly sought profit ratios might otherwise show today.

One hears of "successful" company managers, who produce sparkling profits on the strength of which they move to greater things, by promotion or by being headhunted. Sometimes their companies sink into oblivion a year or two later, in reality because the future had been neglected, yet supposedly "proving" that the success remains only as long as the manager who "created" it. Similarly, a new broom may appear to have produced great improvements, which were in the pipeline all the time.

But what of the questions we have yet to ask, assuming that the answers to the earlier management criteria are found to be favourable?

- Is the sparkling profit ratio calculated after writing off the cost of an adequate research and development programme, to keep ahead of competitors?
- Is the R&D being aimed at markets which are going to require the products being developed – five years after the investment?
- Should the R&D be supported by outside expertise in universities or partner companies that are better qualified?
- Does the product plan take advantage of known and anticipated movements in technology?
- Is the timescale for research, development, design, tooling, production engineering and product launch realistic?
- Will the company's present markets still be there in five years?
- Should the company really be moving into different markets, or should it add a wider range of products to enhance its leverage in the existing ones?
- Should the emphasis on exports, technology transfer or overseas investment be increased?
- Is the company sufficiently vertically integrated, or is it already too dependent on its own singular resources?
- Has the company looked at these questions and does the board have a clear plan of action, in the light of the relevant answers?

- Does the company's management structure allow for executing the plan effectively and are the necessary personal skills available or being sought?

- Is the investment being sought because of insufficient funds for the current business, or because a credible plan to develop the company requires funding to ensure or to speed its success?

Perhaps this last question is the most important one of all.

Only with sufficient positive answers to such questions can a measure of a company's success be estimated. To value a company's shares, or the chief executive's performance, these questions need to considered by those who have experienced the problems of making it happen and who have suffered some of the mistakes inevitably made on the way.

There are few, if any simple answers to the measurement of success. The final proof of the pudding is in the eating and the sweetest prize for the entrepreneur is if he can make the financial gain, which his efforts have created.

In summary

1 Success cannot be measured by the accounting figures alone.

2 Is the company creating the conditions for future success?

3 It takes hands on experience to recognise the difference.

4 To what extent would the investment be a substantial risk?

5 The value of a company is finally determined by what a buyer will pay.

11

AVOIDING END-GAME PITFALLS

Avoiding End-game Pitfalls

Taking on a business shambles and turning it into a fast-moving success is enormously satisfying but look out for pitfalls and lurking dangers

Nobody becomes more involved in his business, or more attached to it, than the entrepreneur who created it from nothing. Perhaps after striving to rescue an insolvent shambles and after surviving on the cash flow knife-edge for years without new funds, while turnover multiplies and loss turns to net profit the entrepreneur cannot be other than emotionally committed. His dedication and enthusiasm rub off on the whole workforce. Even if this has grown into a large team, each knows the other and both take a pride in the achievement. All the brainstorming sessions over new designs, the weeks of travelling the globe, the gentle persuasion of bankers to maintain the overdraft – they all seem worth while when a good reputation has been established; the point when not only customers (at last) bang on the door, but investors make approaches.

Expansion at 30% to 40% annually cannot go on indefinitely without more working capital – even with very healthy margins. Now, assuming that a large source of funds lies behind the controlling shareholder, the entrepreneur who saved the original investment from going down the drain may surely then expect ready finance for the next big leap.

> ***Here beginneth the first lesson***
> ***Don't rely on business logic, especially when yours is a small business among much larger investments.***

If another investor now appears and is attracted by what has been created, he may offer to inject equity to strengthen the balance sheet. The original financier, preoccupied with bigger things, could be delighted to revert to a minority interest and to reduce his stake. His caution or disinterest may have already led to his undervaluing the company, to around the balance sheet (or roughly liquidation) value, and so the majority is up for a song. But to take the majority stake in a galloping modestly profitable company may still require a sum beyond the immediate reach of the entrepreneur. Of course, he would really like to control the business he has created in his own image.

Second lesson
If you have faith in your company and in your own abilities – having come this far, raise the cash yourself.

This is easier said than done, but the entrepreneur should try every possibility, including a second mortgage on his house. Even a consortium of (hopefully) trustworthy friends may be preferable, leaving nobody with the magic 51%, with the entrepreneur retaining sufficient equity and options to back his management control. If all such efforts have been to no avail, the new investor's offer of a cash injection for majority control, may nevertheless flatter the entrepreneurial ego. But what are the new investor's objectives? How will he work with you? And will he really allow you the freedoms which enabled you to build the company in which your life is wholly enmeshed?

So long as you know everything about the business and he is new to it, you will be virtually indispensable, and he will make a deal designed to keep you happy – at least to ensure long enough continuity to cover the possibility that you don't hit it off together. As with all personality matters, nobody can ever foresee how a relationship will develop; so the details of shareholders' agreements and service agreements are vital. A good lawyer may help to protect your interests, but remember that, in the end, it becomes very painful to enforce legal documents through the courts. If it is possible to obtain a complete and independent check of the investor's track record before agreeing to his controlling 'your' baby, you will not regret the effort. Unfortunately, this is not easy. Perhaps it is then best to trust your first instincts.

Third lesson
If you are at all doubtful, say 'No'.

If there is no substantive company search or other financial data to back the investor's claim that he has available funds for the company's future needs – beware. The prospective investor's appearance and claims of success in themselves do not guarantee that your company's funds are to be carefully preserved. If your service agreement leaves you squarely in charge, remember that a majority shareholder can still squeeze you out if he wants to run the business himself – or in his own way. In a private company, shareholders' agreements usually require the minority shareholder (i.e. you, the original entrepreneur) to enter into an option agreement allowing your shares to be acquired by the majority shareholder if you ever leave the company. The price at which these shares would pass will determine whether or not you reap the capital reward for your labours of love. It is absolutely vital to gain satisfactory terms while you have the negotiating power and use it to protect your future.

Fourth lesson
In case you should you ever leave the company, a share option agreement must include your 'Put Option' on the major shareholder, requiring him to buy your shares – at whatever price he might offer to take your shares using his 'Call Option'.

The price terms should:

i Be in direct proportion to the total equity value, specifically excluding any reduction reflecting the fact that your holding is a minority.

ii Give you the right to buy out the majority shareholder at a share price equal to any price he offers for your shares.

iii Specify the company valuation to be on a going concern basis including goodwill, as opposed to the very conservative auditors' valuation, which is usually nearer to liquidation value.

iv State a minimum price per share (e.g. at par).

v If a price/earnings formula is specified, or where any profit or shareholders' funds criteria are specified, make explicit conditions, excluding costs charged to the company by the potential purchaser of your shares.

It is all too easy for a director who is the majority shareholder to spend your company's money, so reducing its value and that of the minority entrepreneur's shares. This leaves you on a hiding to nothing. Profit performance will be reduced and subject to criticism by the very shareholder who spent excessively; the balance sheet and your borrowing power will suffer; and in the event of selling out, the share valuation will have been reduced.

In this respect, a sign of the future may appear during the negotiations for the new investor's acquisition. He may pay for expensive investigations by accountants and management consultants, as well as incurring the legal costs of a reconstruction. If every penny of these costs is then to be claimed out of company funds, this may be the portent of things to come. On the other hand, if an investor bears the costs of his own professional advisers, he is likely to protect your company's funds in other ways for the benefit of all shareholders, including you. Similarly, an investor wishing to stimulate the growth of the company (and of your share value within it) by injecting funds will not take the funds straight back in management fees. Any propensity for charging fees and expenses may signal less than unselfish motives.

Fifth Lesson
A shareholders' agreement which spells out the maximum expenses to be incurred by each must be enforced to the letter, and not just let ride.

Now, after possibly a lonely period as the driving force, it may well be a welcome relief to have a non-executive chairman of proven financial success with whom to discuss ideas and to consult over difficult decisions. This increasingly close business relationship may well lead to the non-executive chairman taking an ever-expanding role in the company. There is a fine dividing line between a very interested non-executive and a chairman who likes to take over the reins.

Sixth lesson
Never allow any blurring of a chief executive's authority.

It is better to be black or white on this issue. If your authority continues to be undermined, square up by invoking your service agreement, before you are blamed for performance, which is not properly under your control. Better to force the issue and risk being sacked with compensation; the later the issue is left, the less likely it is to be resolved in your favour.

In any normal society, however, it is not necessary to spend time looking over one's shoulder. A managing director certainly has enough to do without allowing mental distraction from his full commitment to the success of his company. However, some acts are correct, and some are clearly suspect, or against your reasonable interests. It is always best to face these openly as soon as the evidence is strong enough for you to be sure. The right time may be when you feel that your own integrity is really at stake. If open discussion with an offending party does not result in rapid correction, make sure that proper diary notes are kept both of facts and of conversations attempting to rectify the facts. You may have to address your views and requests for changes in writing to the major shareholder. While this tends to be provocative, it may be necessary to choose between your integrity, reputation and self-respect and a quiet life with subsequent regrets. If directness brings matters to a head, once you need to go this far, so be it.

Few cancers in business are more destructive than company politics, easily started from the top and only eliminated by determined action at the top. In large companies, politics tend to be prevalent and can dominate the expenditure of middle management energies. This must greatly reduce the effectiveness and therefore the profitability of a company; but the momentum of a large organization and of outside influences can keep the ship plodding along. In a small company though, the effect can be quickly disastrous. That is why the first meeting with a team of managers should spell out an absolutely firm rule: No politics. An open relationship at all levels enables most differences to be settled by the parties concerned. If differences have to be settled by higher management, openness and mutual loyalty will overcome the disappointment of a lost argument. You should keep notes on any issues which may threaten your professional reputation, particularly if you sense a danger of future litigation.

Seventh lesson
Never allow or indulge in company politics at any level.

A service agreement with a notice period of a year or more is commonly part of the entrepreneur's package, in his employee capacity. All such agreements tend to favour the employee, since he cannot in practice be held to a notice period longer than about three months; but he is also at some risk. If the employer – in this case his fellow (majority) shareholder decides to dispense with his services, the honourable thing to do (assuming no default or misdeed on the employee's part) is promptly to pay out the full notice period. Otherwise, why enter into such an agreement in the first place? However, an unscrupulous employer may decide effectively to repudiate the contract by simply doing (and paying) nothing, leaving legal action as the only recourse, to recover damages. He knows that legal expenses are high and usually paid (particularly by an unemployed individual) in large advance instalments, before the case ever reaches court. That may mean two years of litigation with an uncertain outcome, before any damages might be paid. Meanwhile, the aggrieved employee/entrepreneur may have forked out £50,000 or much more and wasted a lot of time and emotion in the process.

A sufficiently hard-nosed majority shareholder will expect you to settle for much less than the contract stipulates and you may prefer not to risk the enormous outlay and delay in coming to court. After all, there's always the risk that a judgment may award less than the total provided in the contract and less than the total of legal costs. In fact, the law requires the plaintiff to do all he can to mitigate the damages by obtaining alternative income as soon as possible – otherwise he is held partly responsible for the damages. There is no legal requirement to award damages greater than the actual loss suffered; so a plaintiff with a five-year contract could end up with the equivalent of only six months pay.

> ***Eighth lesson***
> ***A long-term contract may not provide true protection from dismissal. (And as Sam Goldwin famously said –"A verbal contract is not worth the paper it is written on.")***

Not only must the employer keep his word, but the company must have the money to pay the large sum, which corresponds to a long-term contract; a favourable judgment could be worthless if in your absence, the owners of the company allow it to decline. In the case of a limited company, the owners will escape liability if the company cannot pay – unless fraud or a similar crime concerned with deliberately extracting funds from the company can be proved. Such fraudulent activity is difficult to prove to a court, which does not like to entertain fraud charges in civil suits and puts the onus to prove even strong evidence entirely on the plaintiff.

A dispute can arise if profits are reduced by excessive costs incurred by a major shareholder. These are difficult to prevent, when the costs are presented as normal overhead expenses; the auditors may not find anything abnormal. Since lower profits not only provide a stick with which to beat the managing director for "his" poor performance, but also reduce the value of his shares, it is essential to maintain financial control records in sufficient detail to show what went into the broader-brush statutory accounts.

Ninth lesson

Keep records of budgets, account details and other important documents at home: just in case you find yourself sacked and your office files surreptitiously removed.

There can in fact be much unpleasantness in shareholder relationships if they go sour. If the time ever comes to take legal advice, a full set of records produces a ready case history and evidence in the (undesirable) event of litigation. It is essential to be completely frank and open with good legal advisers, if they are to give the best help. *However, lawyers can misjudge business situations, so any vital decisions must remain your own.*

Is there any way in which the minority-holding entrepreneur can rid himself of an all-powerful majority owner, if he feels he is being taken for a ride? He won't want to part with his creation, or his livelihood, or his hopes of realising a well-deserved capital gain. The majority shareholder probably has to be tempted out voluntarily. One way is to find a different partner, backer or purchaser who will value the creation's prospects and your management skills highly enough to offer a tempting price. The necessary contacts around industry and commerce, which result from building a business over some years, mean that it is usually possible to find interested buyers – if the business is as attractive as you think. Given the danger of employees becoming disturbed by premature rumours, it is important to enhance confidentiality by avoiding discussions, if you can, with direct competitors or customers. However, if a formal offer can be obtained at a clearly attractive price, when shareholders are in dispute, the offer may well prove irresistible. Even if an offer is refused, at least it will have the effect of placing a valuation on the company and the entrepreneur's shares.

People who have high integrity prefer not to work behind anybody's back. It follows that, if matters are already coming to a head, the intention to offer a buy-out should be discussed openly with the majority shareholder, even though the act of interesting potential buyers would be the entrepreneur's confidential work. If the major shareholder is predatory, this discussion is likely to provide a good indication of his price – an obvious advantage when talking to likely buyers for your firm. Confidentiality is the most important and the most difficult thing to preserve in these circumstances. So the fewer people who know, the better. A man whose life is bound up with the business will in any case take great care only to contemplate a deal which also protects his management team and all employees. Nevertheless, once politics have been injected into an otherwise loyal team, there are great dangers. Even close team members, whose senior positions were created out of your efforts, and who have apparently excellent relationships with you, may harbour ambition or resentment of strong leadership, which could lead to what you would interpret as disloyalty.

A prospective buyer will almost certainly make it a condition of a deal that the original entrepreneur stays with the company, to maintain the drive and the vision which made it an attractive prospect in the first place. This will be very gratifying; but remember that there may be some who think differently, or who would like to mastermind competitive deals. No deal is therefore certain until the ink is dry on the contracts; not even when all details have been agreed and the main parties have shaken hands over the draft documents fresh from the lawyers. If a deal fails at such a stage, the fat is likely to be in the fire; again, the need for confidentiality is paramount, in case personal ambition tempts somebody to block the deal.

> ***Tenth lesson***
> ***Trust nobody but those who absolutely must be party to an acquisition deal: put those on notice in writing about their obligation for maintaining confidences and request their confirmation.***

This catalogue of dangers, warnings and lessons may give the aspiring entrepreneur the impression that it is not worth it. Nothing is further from the truth. Immense satisfaction arises from creating an interesting and growing business, from having the power of decision over market and product developments and from winning the hearts (and payments) of willing customers. This is further enhanced if a loyal team of managers and other workers has been created. The free market system alone can provide these opportunities, and a shareholding in a growing asset under your control is the surest ways to personal wealth.

Eleventh lesson

Try to keep at least 51% and if this is not possible, make sure that no other sole shareholder acquires a majority.

Minority institutional shareholders are one possible route. They won't always make efforts to protect an entrepreneurial partner. But with them you do at least have a better chance.

Here endeth the lessons.

12

POSTSCRIPT – ENTREPRENEURIAL EXPECTATIONS

Postscript – Entrepreneurial Expectations

If I can be excused a personal reflection, this chapter provides one that could nevertheless be of interest to budding entrepreneurs.

It has been said, that to "make it", one should be able to bank the first million by the age of 21. This is much easier in Italian lire than in Sterling or US dollars, so most entrepreneurs have to remain content with much less, even when they retire – if they ever do. In the United States, there are over one million millionaires, one for every hundred households. Even l'il ol' Georgia, long perceived (by those who do not know the South) as a slow thinking State with high levels of poverty and rural "rednecks", boasts nearly fifteen thousand of them.

Who would have thought that the friendly Po Folks restaurants where they serve coffee in Mason Jars and the menus are written in Southern phonetic joke language would convert a $5,000 investment into a $15m sale after only eight years?

People seem to make a good living from the strangest of occupations. Some examples make an engineer-trained late developer think wryly, how much more easily others seem to make substantial bucks, than by worrying about esoteric technical matter, global pricing policy, national approvals and industrial management problems. Although my uncle owned a restaurant near Trafalgar Square and I was allowed into the kitchen to raid the sizzling chip pans when my parents worked there during the Blitz in World War II, my inclinations and training could never have led me into catering or retail. Yet the stories of Conrad Hilton, Bill Marriott, Charles Forté and Philip Green make me wonder why I went into engineering. Not that modern catering and world-class hotels are short of technical or management challenges. Perhaps the difference lies in the very basic nature of a hot dog and soda stand – and the supposedly more intellectually demanding world of (say) aircraft and electronics. The real entrepreneur thinks more of the reality of an opportunity, than of its nature. If the market will pay for a product or a service, exploit the opportunity. The simpler the good idea, the less starting capital it is likely to need and the more likely will fourteen hours of hard work per day for six days a week convert it into a fortune. 80% of the million American millionaires are aged sixty-nine and worked their way to their fortunes at that rate.

Looking back, when at nearly forty after a career of employment in large companies, I was offered my chance to make real money in engineering, my wife refused to believe my expectations. I could have total freedom to develop a company on mainly others' capital, with a modest equity stake as incentive. It was an opportunity too good to miss. After all, when a company is on the verge of going out of business, if it does not crash immediately, things can only improve. I was convinced that my shares would eventually be worth at least half of that magic million, after five or six years, but my wife's scepticism proved to be right on two counts. In the first place, it took much longer than I had expected; secondly, although my entrepreneurial efforts and those of the team I assembled earned enough on selling the company, to value my stake at well over the magic million in Sterling, virtually all of it went to the major shareholder, who took care to see that I was out of the way in good time. Without the controlling share in an enterprise, perhaps I was not the first to prove that I could make a million, but that I could also lose it to those better equipped with starting funds and brass necks.

On the other hand, many minority shareholding entrepreneurs manage to keep hold of their hard earned rewards, so it would be wrong to be unduly cynical about entrepreneurial expectations. It is more a question of differentiating between the success of an enterprise and the success of a personal outcome. It is easy to become so absorbed and committed to the creative process, in which the enterprise and its daily progress become everything, that the entrepreneur may naively forget that his personal outcome is not the first priority of others. Unless it is his own first priority, he relies too much on honesty and goodwill all around. These conditions are sadly in rather short supply. The "my brains and your money" combination may be all very well, as far as it goes in a fair world, but "my brains and my money" is a safer bet.

Financial expectations provide the carrot for entrepreneurs, but when their lives are compared with those of well paid executives in big corporations, other factors may be even more important in the long run. Lifestyles tend to revolve around the choice between working to live, or living to work. It is rightly said, that the man who works for himself, works the hardest. This is often as true of the completely independent entrepreneur as it is for the chief executive who generally writes his own timetable, but nevertheless answers to a boss or fellow shareholders. But the independence of being one's own boss, even if a big fish in a small puddle bears no comparison with the restrictions and daily pressures experienced by the biggest tycoon in the greatest corporation. Public company stock market and shareholder pressures leave little room for truly entrepreneurial minds to run free. If there is a layer or more of corporate structure between a five thousand employee division's board chairman and a group board, he remains the meat in the sandwich. The pressures from above added to the self-generated ones leave little room for changes in direction or for rapid, decision making.

The big corporations are the antithesis of most entrepreneurs' expectations, due to the bureaucracy and the politics so often endemic to them. Only recently has there been much written in the business school and management media about fostering entrepreneurism and leadership in corporations, as opposed to departmentalised management and administrative skills. So, except for the entrepreneur who has become so successful that he has grown his own empire and remained at the apex, they hardly exist outside smaller businesses. Furthermore, no longer does the large established corporation assure stability of employment, even for top executives. The entrepreneur is mostly on a knife-edge and dreams of building a secure future. Yet there are examples galore, of successful corporate executives being heaved out of their panelled offices, in mergers, reorganisations, market downturns or merely boardroom brawls.

Is it better to live high on a large salary and expenses, with a fortune in stock options and to trade up gradually from ulcers to heart attacks, or at the other end of the scale, to turn one's hand to everything from negotiating acquisitions to wrapping parcels? It is always greener on the other side of the fence and both lifestyles have their advantages and their problems. Having seen or tasted both lifestyles, I feel the pull of the free spirit, even though an entrepreneur should never close the door to an offer nobody can refuse.

The ideal situation of the free spirit, who makes so much money that he can live high, but can still finish up as the richest man in the cemetery may be at the end of a rainbow. Yet the expectations of those who are entrepreneurs at heart reach all the way to that goal. High expectations help to keep them young and justify their occasional flamboyance. After all, a fortune is not much use under six feet of earth. Why not a Bentley on American low octane fuel? Why not keep the airlines in business, with transatlantic travel for the whole family? Why not choose, which months to be in Europe and when to be in America? There is nobody to say "No" and we always have the expectation of reaching that pot of gold, while we are young enough to enjoy it.

Additional thoughts for small business entrepreneurs

1 Don't wait for bankers, who rarely understand much besides risk.

2 It isn't always best to trust the advice of lawyers, accountants and other "experts". Get professional help in any area where you are lacking – but trust your own instincts.

3 Never be too proud to admit – to yourself or to others – when you have made a mistake. "A man who never made a mistake never made anything!"

4 Take advice from your spouse and try to maintain a consensus on major business policies.

APPENDIX

Appendix

The Managing Director's Sleepless Night

THANK goodness that's organised! If I hold up for two weeks plus, covering the usual ten cities coast to coast, all will be well – as long as not too many of my appointments are changed, cancelled or forgotten by hosts with their own priorities. Still, it is three months since my last 'rounds' and this time I do have some sort of confirmation from all but Chicago and San Diego. I only hope that this lot turns out to be nearer the mark than some on the last trip. It seems that one out of ten potential partners survives three visits if I e-mail and fax frequently enough between trips and spend fortunes on transatlantic calls – usually in the middle of dinner. The ace is to get one over to England for more than thirty six hours. Then he is usually serious enough and there is the chance of making a deal.

It is as well that as MD I can at least take decisions at any meeting. Otherwise when I send somebody else, however senior, some damned obstacle has to be cleared when I am in Saudi Arabia or Cairo where telephones take longer to connect. Then the steam just subsides and it is like starting all over again.

Had to rebook the itinerary three times – my secretary nearly gave in her notice, and even now I have large sections of my ticket open. I shall have to hassle the reservations as I go along. It may well add 50 per cent to the fare, but we'll have to turn a blind eye to that and hope that I can stick with economy fares without losing any of my connections. What would I do without credit cards? And what would I do without a large and a small briefcase and strong biceps? The problem will be like LA the last time, when I'll probably make the Phoenix flight by the skin of my teeth and have to run all the way to the gate carrying all of my bags.

Once every two or three months is bad enough; what will it be like when we are actually getting the business going – finding a factory, negotiating a lease, hiring staff, training distributors, placing advertising, keeping the bank happy, clearing shipping documents, dealing with late deliveries and faulty packing, agreeing extra test requirements? All will be well once I can afford to budget for a more experienced chap on the team in America. But for some months I'll have to hold this baby myself. This is not one of those cases where my Sales Director (bless his fiery soul) can negotiate the joint venture contract and run the show for our side. He would be dealing with an aggressive American president with twenty years of general management behind him. We even had problems running a selling operation until I increased the frequency of my visits.

Still, I have a couple of days till Friday to clear the March management accounts and to approve the new technical literature. On yes, must be sure to squeeze in a few hours to clear the engineering progress meeting. Otherwise that programme will be four weeks behind by the time I return. Production had better make its budgeted deliveries this month. Pity I could not delay the trip till after month end, to help keep the pressure on. Perhaps I should make a tactful phone call from New York before my breakfast meeting next Friday. If I make it soon after 5 a.m., I'll catch the works director just after his progress meeting. (I'll also ask him to phone the wife to let her know when I expect to arrive back.)

Must get it all together Friday afternoon, including papers for all meetings, new product specifications, that draft licence agreement and – oh yes, must go over that with those damned lawyers. She will kill me if I go into the office on Saturday when I'm leaving on Sunday for two weeks. I would really like to make an extra week while I am over there, but I must be back for the AGM and board meetings. Perhaps I'll find a quiet seat with nobody near enough to keep talking to me. That will give me four or five hours between meals, to go over all the papers and to write that article for the trade journal. I could also prepare for the board meeting, as there will be too much report writing to do on the homeward flight. It is as well that I cannot sleep on airplanes.

Where can I find another 'me'?

If only I could be in two places at once. I would stay over there and concentrate on the US scene. Even 50 per cent of my time for six months would be worth twenty trips. Then my alter ego could spend the other 100 per cent running the rest of the company and keeping the other markets moving. The business would move faster and surer. We could soon afford to hire a really experienced president for the American operation and he could really move it along. I would only need to keep in touch on vital matters and perhaps visit once or twice per year.

But where can I find another 'me', who has done it all successfully before and whom I can trust? I may only need him for a few months and if he were constantly accessible right there, I would not even have to pay him full time. The trouble is that people like that are probably running a company full time already.

If I could find that alter ego, I would brief him thoroughly on the company, the products and our objectives and limitations. Then I would send 'me' out to 'my' wide range of US contacts and find three or four really likely partners.

If he is already set up in the US, I would not even have to send him and he would be in better contact still with the market. He could evaluate companies, thoroughly report back, then open negotiations and present me with a draft heads of agreements which would be likely to be acceptable to both sides. Then I could close the deal on the next trip. After which I could prevail on him to hire my top man from a position of knowledge and to keep an eye on things for me on a part time basis. Probably would cost less than all these trips and I would have time to make sure we have a profit on all of our operations. Where can I find another 'me' for a few months? Come to think of it, BOTB did tell me of a chap who set up in Atlanta. Said to be a real communications hub in the US. I hope I remember to ask them about him in the morning.

John Forbat

Article appeared in *Commerce International*, June, 1982.

Index

D

E

G

I

L

M

N

O

P

R

S

T

V